BATTLE OF THE WHITE APARTMENTS

A STORY OF THE SURGE

JB GARRISON

NEWMAN SPRINGS PUBLISHING
320 Broad Street
Red Bank, NJ 07701

First originally published by Newman Springs Publishing 2021

ISBN 978-1-63692-239-3 (Paperback)
ISBN 978-1-63692-240-9 (Digital)

Printed in the United States of America

Bombing, particularly on the receiving end, is not "communication." Bombs result in death and destruction.

—Lieutenant General H. R. McMaster

To S.Sgt. Bradley King, awarded the Bronze Star, Purple Heart, and Army Commendation medals, a great soldier, superior mechanic, and great friend, rest in glorious peace, brother.

To all of the wounded warriors of the 152nd Infantry and Team Ready First. You were simply the best of all bests. Serving with you all was simply an honor and true privilege. Thank you.

And especially to my treasured daughter, Hannah Jo, it was harder on you than it was on me.

CONTENTS

INTRODUCTION

Early fall, during the fall of October 2006 a gaggle of 152 Infantrymen from the Indiana Army National Guard's Company A, Second Battalion of the 152nd Infantry Regiment joined the War on Terror. Alpha Company had been given the deployment order six months earlier and were sent to Iraq, to serve in what was called "Operation Iraqi Freedom". The 152nd, now very far away from their home state of Indiana, took the quick and dangerous two-hour flight from Kuwait and was then ordered by corps headquarters to the far west side of Baghdad, to join the Ninety-Second Military Police Battalion at the dusty and rugged "Camp Liberty".

Many of the soldiers in our company were freshly out of basic training. Following basic training meant nine additional weeks of Infantry training at the Army's home of the Infantry, Fort Benning, located in humid, steamy southern Georgia. Fort Benning is the charm of the Army, training and producing the "ultimate weapon", the American Infantry Soldier. And that is what we were deployed with, over 100 ultimate weapons.

Some of the Infantrymen in our company were only 18 or 19 years of age. These youthful soldiers watched in fear during the 9/11 attacks that were inflicted on American soil from televisions mounted on school history and algebra classroom walls on that horrible Monday morning that seemed to stop the world from turning, as evil grasped the western hemisphere. Children sat in silence as the

New York City's twin towers collapsed, and cringed as the southern outer corridor of the Pentagon was set ablaze by another cowardly attack that day. Word later spread of a missing plane, somewhere heading westward over Pennsylvania or possibly Ohio, and was it heading toward Indianapolis the teenagers probed as they continued to stare at the dreadful images? Indianapolis was a metropolis that many of the kids' parents worked everyday, and a place that many of the kids' relatives lived and called home.

Many of the kids knew, once finished with high school, joining the Army or Marine Corps was their calling. Perhaps a calling that was more of a stand against the newly found enemies of the free world. These new warriors raised their right hands, swore an allegiance to the Constitution... to fight against all enemies, both foreign and domestic. And that was a loyal oath to fight for America and its home land, a land that had recently been attacked and charred that September morning.

America had once again been attacked without warning or notice... an attack that mirrored the meaningless attacks on Pearl Harbor in December of 1941. The children that morning stared in terror, much like their grandparents and great-grandparents did during the beginning of World War II as Hawaii burned. These were horrible images that mirrored the Japanese bombing that late Indiana summer morning, a September morning that was pleasantly sunny yet cool, a perfect harvest temperature of 68 degrees. The kids gazed at the horrific images in New York and Washington DC, exactly as the world saw the many ships, such as the USS Arizona, and the Hawaiian naval base in total chaos some 60 years earlier.

The teens soon graduated, and joined up. Joined as so many other Americans did during the Vietnam war, both World Wars, Korea. Now, they were in Iraq to serve, fight and survive in a strange, rustic and forsaken place that they knew very little about.

A new war was on, the War on Terror. Coalition forces began pouring into Afghanistan, and later invaded the country of Iraq in 2002. American youth joined in masses, and generals began the delicate and precise planning for war. A global war that encircled the middle east.

Our unit was tasked to do the military police's dirty work on the western side of Baghdad. And in our eyes, that was our job as the sole combat unit in a noncombat battalion against a ruthless and merciless enemy, and enemy sworn to the core to defeat the Westerners who had invaded their homeland four years earlier that had recently declared victory over the Islamic country.

Our primary job was to go into the battle, find the fight and win. After receiving word of a disabled coalition vehicle, a team from the 152nd would be dispatched to perform recovery detail, even if it was in the midst of an attack, counterattack, or follow-on ambush. The fellas trapped knew one thing was on their side and soon on the way, a response and recovery team.

But duty in Baghdad did not last long for our Hoosier company. We would soon be working, living, and fighting in the southern section of the Iraqi "Triangle of Death," specifically in the Al Anbar providence's town of Ar Ramadi that skirted the Syrian border.

April of 2005, the 152nd Regiment had completed a one-year tour of duty in Bosnia and six months later was in New Orleans assisting with relief efforts from Hurricanes Katrina and Rita that destroyed New Orleans and the Gulf areas. But this current mission would be a completely different tasking for our infantry company. A massive troop build-up was forming for troubled Iraq that was spinning out of control with hundreds of Americans being killed and seriously wounded by a new, invisible threat by the Insurgency in Iraq... the Improvised Explosive Device, or "IED". Highly skilled snipers were also added to the theater threat against coalition forces. Snipers trained in nearby Syria and Iran to cause fear and death in Iraq.

Coalition was hated with a deep passion and striking fear and tragedy in the region was pressed hard and quick. Washington demanded answers. Generals, politicians and skilled civilians joined forces to create a resolution in 2006. And this remedy enflamed the sitting commanding general in charge of the Iraqi war. But decisions were made and orders were published. The Iraqi surge was on.

A barrage of five combat brigades added to the fight in Iraq was forming from within the deep, dark chambers of the Pentagon, and the president and congress gambled on this enormous plan. A plan that would place a huge responsibility of redirecting the war's troubled direction, with heavy pressure placed in the laps of units such as ours, Alpha Company of the 152 Infantry Regiment. A push of more Americans were needed to assist the Iraqi Police and Iraqi Army to succeed in order to return victory in coalition hands, and someday depart the middle-eastern country plagued by years of war, deception, and a destroyed economy.

This story is based on true events. Names of soldiers in the unit have been changed for privacy.

Our unit was Alpha Company of the 152nd Infantry Regiment, a regiment from the Thirty-Eighth Infantry Division, Indiana Army National Guard. Our infantry unit was based out of Indianapolis, the "Cyclone Soldiers". And I was the company executive officer. My call-name, "Cyclone-5", I was Cyclone-5.

THE LANDING

The flight into Baghdad International Airport was just as horrible as it could possibly be. The landing was what was known as a combat landing, arriving in stealth mode at night into the heart of war-torn Baghdad. Without aircraft lights, the C-130 cargo air force pilot raised, lowered, sped up, slowed down, and dipped his craft into the darkness in search of the massive Baghdad airstrip. Following what seemed hours of a horrible flight experience, our infantry company somehow and miraculously safely landed onto the center runway of the once known Saddam International Airport. The taxi to the cargo docks seemed to last an eternity, yet we were prepared for combat. We were prepared for any firefight, battle, or war at this point. We were ready for anything. We were the 152nd Infantry, the cyclones of the battlefield. We were ready for anything at any cost in any way.

As the gigantic rear door of the now grounded Air Force Hercules quickly dropped, our National Guard Infantry unit of 152 guys finally stepped foot for the first time on Iraqi soil. We had prepared for this moment for six months that began at our Indianapolis home station that later included training at Fort Dix for two exhausting, grueling months during the humid summer months of July and August of 2006. We had spent months from family and friends, personal freedom and relax. But now, finally here in the combat zone. Something we honored yet feared. But we were here in Baghdad. In theater, ready for anything at this moment and prepared to meet our unit that we were prepared to replace and relieve of duty in Baghdad. We were ready for anything at all.

Following our time at Fort Dix, we spent three blistering weeks in Kuwait for final preparation for duty in Iraq. Now we were finally here in Baghdad.

The C-130 aircraft hummed as we shuffled out of the bird's cargo area as quickly as we possibly could. Orders were barked, bags off-loaded, while weapons and personnel were closely accounted for. This is something that had been preached about for months during our buildup for this mission in Iraq, leadership and accountability. And after finally arriving in Iraq after months and months of what seemed endless training, the fear of the unknown quickly set in for our infantry company. Within minutes, our gear and troops were swiftly hustled off the dark noisy Baghdad flight line into a makeshift waiting area made of cement freeway barriers. A few short minutes later, the C-130 aircraft that the United States military have heavily relied on since the Vietnam war quickly revved its four propeller engines and blasted off into the dark Baghdad night.

Our unit was alerted ten months prior to our arrival to Baghdad of the possible deployment to either Iraq or Afghanistan. We were not exact on the final destination for our Hoosier Infantry unit. But an alert in these times for the military were not tests or training drills in any way. Alerts meant start packing, get personal matters taken care of, and prep for a long and slow dragging year away from home and family. Most importantly, be prepared to soon be in harm's way. The war on terror was entering its sixth year, and our number was up for an unknown combat deployment in the Middle East.

Our unit's lush home drilling station at Stout Field located on the west side of Indianapolis quickly changed to the remote and secluded Camp Atterbury national guard training center, a rustic military compound that quietly housed sixty-five weapon ranges and eighteen very harsh training sites. Atterbury was not too far away from Indianapolis, and this historic camp was recently dedicated by the Department of Defense to return as a key mobilization base, to now train units going to Iraq, Afghanistan, Kosovo, and beyond. Atterbury, covering several hundred acres of land, is a gigantic base where military training dates back to World War II. The camp is settled in the thick woods of south-central Indiana, and Atterbury was perfect for our initial training and preparation for Alpha's upcoming combat deployment supporting the international war on terror...a deployment that we senior 152 leaders were unsure of at this stage of our alert order.

The National Guard was a lifesaver for the Department of Defense following the 9/11 attacks. America's active duty military had been stretched as thin as it could possibly handle with massive operations in Iraq, Afghanistan, and elsewhere around the world, and the guard and reserve forces were pulling a large load. And it was just a matter of time for soldiers to get an alert while in the reserve forces. Our time was now.

For the very first time, it dawned on me as we were staged at the edge of the Baghdad International Airport that the entire unit of infantry-hardened men was near silent. And it was a very strange silent. Breaking the quiet, two low-flying Black Hawk helicopters caught my eye from the far east side of the airport, and the pair hovered over the flight line with blinding spotlights mounted under the belly of each craft. My guess was the duo were completing a security check on and around the many runways of the airstrip or checking for debris, trash, or stalled service vehicles that could interfere with one of the many C-130 or 17s landing in complete darkness. The spotlights were as bright as day, reminding me of the movie I watched in awe as a kid, *Close Encounters of the Third Kind*, with monstrous lights beaming down to the earth as people watched with amazement. I could not get my attention away from the Black Hawks as our bags and boxes loaded cargo trucks bound for yet another staging area as we waited for someone, anyone, to instruct us where to go next.

The current security threat remained high for aircraft arriving and departing in Baghdad although coalition forces maintained a strong grip of security throughout the country. As blasting winds and piercing dust was kicked up by the pair of Black Hawks, it was only an everyday event on that busy Baghdad flight line. But we managed to keep alert and focused during the confusion and noise that night as midnight arrived.

The pair of Black Hawks soon disappeared into the distance. Then senior leaders searched for answers of where to go next in the dark. We needed heavy equipment to move our equipment and some form of transportation to get our troops to nearby Camp Liberty. One of my favorite squad leaders, Richard Ray, quickly jumped to security mode and ordered his squad to scan front, left, and right for any possible enemy sneak attack. But to Ray's surprise, the only sneak attack was a pair of American female airmen strolling by, wearing fatigue pants, T-shirts with military issued boots, and of course, a mandatory reflector belt. Were we overdressed? Maybe overstressed? In passing, the airmen laughed at us if saying, "Welcome, new guys…"

I had known Ray for years and always called Ray "Richie." Ray was a 1993 Somali vet with the 101st Airborne Division and very trusted by our command leadership. Ray looked at me as the airmen walked by our gaggle and sighed. "How embarrassing."

We spent the first month of our tour in the Baghdad area at Camp Liberty that was located on the far west side of the massive city. We were assigned to the Ninety-Second Military Police Battalion. They were also based at Camp Liberty. The Ninety-Second fell under the Eighty-Ninth Military Police Brigade, and the Eighty-Ninth answered directly to the theater corps commander that was located not too far away at Camp Victory. Camp Victory could easily be seen from our side of the enormous military compound, and corps headquarters was within walking distance from Liberty. Corps headquarters was a fantastic place to visit when given the chance. Corps sat directly in the middle of Camp Victory and was complete with a strangely shaped man-made lake, formed in an odd Z shape that spanned two football fields. The lake was formed next to a huge palace that corps claimed for itself following the coalition invasion of 2002. The palace towered over one hundred feet tall and protected by a small moat. Camp Victory also had three smaller palaces that at one time housed high-ranking Iraqi military leaders who were related to or highly trusted by Saddam.

Construction of the palaces and Z Lake were very closely supervised by Saddam that began in the early 1990s, and I was told the main palace was originally planned for Saddam's mother to live in. But Saddam was so pleased with the final product he decided to keep the palace for himself. The then Iraqi dictator also had a large eighty-foot statue made of himself to look over western Iraq, facing the Sunni area of the country. Only Saddam's closest family members and high-ranking generals were allowed to visit this spectacle of a military garrison.

Saddam simply adored this enormous compound although his once treasured military headquarters would now house him as a prisoner and eventually tried by his own people…and hung.

The Eighty-Ninth Military Police Brigade, based out of Fort Hood when stateside, was under a dark cloud as we arrived at Camp Liberty. One of the Eighty-Ninth Brigade's subordinate commanders had been recently arrested, and the circumstances turned very ugly. Lt. Col. William Steele had been relieved of command for several disturbing charges that included aiding the enemy and unauthorized possession of classified documents. And the Eighty-Ninth was not proud of the ugly events and spoke rarely of the disgrace at hand.

Lieutenant Colonel Steele, an army reservist from Virginia, had been charged with aiding the enemy while commander of the 451st Military Police Detachment. The 451st was a unit that fell under the Eighty-Ninth at nearby Camp Cropper. Steele served as the senior officer at Camp Cropper from the beginning of October 2005 to the end of October 2006. Cropper was a key coalition holding or detention facility in Iraq for high-level or VIP prisoners to include Saddam Hussein himself.

Steele was eventually acquitted of aiding the enemy. However, the field-grade officer was sentenced to two years confinement on other charges, unauthorized possession of classified documents, behavior unbecoming an officer for an inappropriate relationship with an interpreter, and failing to obey an order.

The troubled officer was also investigated for fraternization with the daughter of a prisoner, a prisoner who was once detained at Camp Cropper while Steele was serving as the camp's commandant. Steele also failed to properly oversee expenditures of government funds while at Cropper.

Surprisingly, Steele was using government funds to purchase hair dyes and Cuban cigars for Saddam Hussein while the former Iraqi dictator was held at Camp Cropper pending trial. The entire situation was very dreadful.

Camp Cropper covered a very small section of the immense complex on Baghdad's west side. Cropper had tall windowless walls that circled the compound. The gray walls stood forty feet tall and edged the south side of the Baghdad International Airport, the airport that ironically once bared Saddam Hussain's name.

The legal process following the allegations did not go well for the disgraced lieutenant colonel. By general court-martial, the highest level of military courts, Steele was later confined to the United States Disciplinary Barracks at Fort Leavenworth, and he was the only field-grade officer to be charged with aiding the enemy during Operation Iraqi Freedom. Steele was also denied of his military retirement, forfeiture of pay, and finally dismissed from the United States Army in disgrace.

DUCK AND COVER

All soldiers in our unit called Indiana Home and proud to be in the second battalion of the 152nd Infantry Regiment. When at home, we answered to the Seventy-Sixth Infantry Brigade of the proud Thirty-Eighth "Cyclone" Infantry Division. Our infantry regiment was richly filled with history that dates back to service during World War II, earning the proud name of the "Avengers of Bataan." The regiment spearheaded the effort to liberate Bataan, saving thousands of lives and making quite a name for itself during the Second World War. The 152nd also led the charge to assist in hurricane relief efforts after Hurricanes Katrina and Rita that destroyed the Mississippi Gulf region one year prior to our dreadful landing in Baghdad. The company was a very close unit that really stuck together and worked well in any condition or environment. We were infantrymen and could take anything and any environment. Grunts that could take anything.

Now we were at Iraq's Camp Liberty to live and work out of medium-sized huts. Not the safest working and living conditions for what was going on in the region, but our huts kept the rain off our heads and dust out of our ears. Overall, it was okay at Liberty.

I was unsure of what our mission with the MP brigade exactly was going to be following our arrival. We were an Army National Guard Infantry combat arms unit and far from military police. But what I did know was that we were to replace the 180th Field Artillery

Battery that was finishing up their Iraqi tour in just over eleven months, and I predicted we would do about the same time, give or take a few weeks.

The 180th loved us. We were their new best friends, their replacements. Returning to Arizona was just a few short weeks away for the 180th, and they rolled out the red carpet for our unit with huge smiles.

After huddling with the leadership of the 180th that first night at Liberty, we were briefed on their current mission and what duties we were to take over. The 152nd commander, Captain Daniel Henton, selected First Platoon to be assigned as security escort and overall security for our new brigade commander. Second Platoon was to assist with vehicle recovery missions in the Baghdad area. Third Platoon was ordered as first responders or more of quick reaction team to cover western Baghdad. Fourth Platoon was detailed to Camp Ramadi, about forty or forty-five miles west of Camp Liberty. Fourth would assist Iraqi Police in Ar Ramadi, a city plagued with violence with a population of 220,000 Sunni Arabs.

On my second day at Camp Liberty, I was offered to tag along with a convoy to travel "outside of the wire." A five-vehicle convoy was loading up to take a quick trip to the Corps' Army Hospital located in what was famously known as the "Green Zone." I had heard of the Green Zone but didn't know much about this mysterious place, except that it was located in downtown Baghdad.

I was eager to convoy through Baghdad with some of the 180th guys, and I quickly became friends with all of them.

I was briefed that the Green Zone was a walled off and highly secured area in central Baghdad. This fortified area housed the Iraqi government, as well as the US embassy. The Green Zone also accommodated a large variety of other important factions of Iraq such as the Ministry of Defense. I was told that prior to our unit's arrival in Iraq, the Green Zone was known as the "International Zone." No one was sure why the name was changed, but the Green Zone was what we were to refer to the secretive compound as.

But tensions were running tight within the Green Zone's gated perimeter. The war was beginning to crumble and slip away from coalition control, and a solution was desperately needed and needed quickly.

The convoy included a few senior officers from brigade who were joining us for the quick trip to the Green Zone and spend a few hours away from the busy and hectic headquarters area that seemed a little overpopulated and chaotic. Tons of inbound and outbound equipment were spread throughout the dusty southeast portion of Camp Liberty for the changeover. Soldiers were everywhere, and a light sandstorm hit the base that morning. Getting away from Liberty and the pandemonium was a good thing for me as well, and I was getting a chance to experience my first tactical convoy through Baghdad.

The Green Zone was not far from Camp Liberty, maybe fifteen to sixteen miles away from camp. This convoy was expected to be a quick and simple voyage to the Green Zone and back, only taking a few hours to complete. Traveling by military convoy required a minimum of four gun trucks. A flawless personnel manifest was mandatory along with a quick inspection prior to departing the perimeter gate.

I sat in the rear passenger seat of the lead gun truck for the trip to the Green Zone. Being stuffed in the back seat of a Hummer was not the most comfortable of rides. The required protective gear that was mandatory to wear made the trip miserable. I quickly found out my gear was new, clean, and very rigid compared to the seasoned Iraqi veteran soldiers' gear. After a year or so of duty in Iraq, uniforms were dull, beat up, dusty, comfortably worn in, and frayed beyond repair. The crew who was escorting me to the Green Zone were very seasoned Iraqi combat veterans with a lot of convoy experience, ready to proudly go home after one year in theater. Following a few weeks in Kuwait and an eighteen-hour flight back to the states meant a possible welcome-home party or a family reunion.

I could not get out of my mind that soldiers in the convoy were wearing dilapidated and tattered uniforms that seemed just as beat and as tired as they were. It was obvious that their tour of duty was very difficult for the soldiers of the 180th. Countless convoys to and from Ramadi, missions throughout Baghdad and Fallujah, nasty dust storms combined with Iraq's vile desert heat had put its toll on the brigade's soldiers.

This convoy to the Green Zone was branded the final mission outside of Victory Base for these guys of the 180th. The mission seemed simple and easy for the combination of soldiers from the 180th and a few from the Eighty-Ninth, very routine, and the route was well-known to them. The light at the end of the deployment tunnel was rapidly approaching, and the newly arrived 152nd Infantry was soon to say goodbye to the 180th Field Artillery guys and take over.

Departing the highly fortified gate of Victory Base was simple. We handed over our convoy's manifest with vehicle information, followed with a quick check of the convoy's weapons, and waved forward to load weapons. The loading of ammunition in the truck's turrets was meticulously supervised by gate staff. A gun nest propped twenty feet high over the entrance provided security against threats, as well as oversight of the area near the vulnerable passageway. Suicide bombers targeted coalition gate entrances; they were weak points to hit. Vehicles used in these vicious attacks were often disguised as ambulances or dump trucks, packed with explosives that produced explosions that could be felt for miles.

Our convoy that day consisted of Hummer gun trucks equipped with .50 caliber Browning M2 machine guns. The Browning could really reach out and cause complete destruction quickly from the trucks. The third Hummer modeled an M249 machine gun, a smaller caliber of bullet, but quick and very powerful. Iraqis feared the American .50 caliber machine gun. They knew the destruction that could be inflicted by the potent weapon.

It only took a few minutes until security gave the final approval to depart the safety of Victory, and we were on our way. This was my much-anticipated maiden voyage off the base, a quick trip through Baghdad that I was very enthusiastic to experience. As our convoy strolled out of the gate and rambled through the west side of Baghdad, the crew of the Hummer I was with was able to point out a few key sites over the truck's intercom. I tried to turn my body in different directions to see the sights of Baghdad, straining to obtain a glimpse of what was being addressed by the convoy commander who was in the front passenger seat.

Sitting in the truck's rear seat, behind the driver, was the safest spot to be in; I was told by the convoy commander. Most IED attacks were directed from the roadside of the truck's passenger side, so sitting behind the driver absorbed the least of an enemy attack. I could also make eye contact with the convoy commander, who was always placed in the front passenger seat of the gun truck.

But I noticed, as our convoy picked up speed, a checkpoint stood approximately two or three miles away from Victory's main gate. But this checkpoint was not manned by Americans; they were Iraqis wearing blue uniforms with AK-47 semiautomatic weapons. Sandbags and plywood were propped against a few cement protective walls that provided a little bit of protection, as well as shade for the Iraqis who were keeping a close eye on the flow of traffic and safety on the highway. It was relieving to see the security detail, but this checkpoint provided meager security compared to the highly fortified Victory main gate. Our convoy slowed. We waved to the checkpoint manned by local security that included an American Hummer that had "Iraqi Army" painted on all possible areas of the truck. The truck had a squad of Iraqi Army soldiers standing nearby as well to strengthen the checkpoint's firepower.

As we trucked a little deeper into Baghdad, I noticed another makeshift checkpoint. But this checkpoint seemed different compared to the Iraqi checkpoints near Victory that had an Iraqi Army infantry squad assigned to it and a few Iraqi policemen. This checkpoint was manned by what seemed to be Pakistani soldiers; a few sandbags were used as speed bumps rather than safety or security for the soldiers manning the lackluster of a roadside checkpoint. The soldiers did not wear any form of protective vests or helmets and were standing in the open at the side of the road. The further we were from our home base of Victory, the skimpier protection.

Several of these skimpy isolated checkpoints were scattered along the highway from Victory to the Corps Hospital. This highway was a main artery for coalition that ran through the heart of Baghdad and branded "Route Irish" that easily lead us to the mysterious Green Zone. As we neared the Green Zone, another checkpoint of Iraqi Police could be seen within a few miles from the compound's main gate. The entrance was littered with concertina wire, massive gray protective walls made of three-foot-thick cement, and fortified towers with machine gun barrels pointed in every possible direction. Warning signs in several languages were plastered on each side of the main gate of the Green Zone, basically stating this was a coalition forces protected area, danger, and stay back five hundred meters. Bright-red signs provided lethal warnings of what could happen to attackers and unauthorized traffic. The entrance into the Green Zone was more of a maze than a gate to navigate through and a challenge to pass through even at a slow speed. Winding corridors with massive barriers and sandbags were placed strategically to ensure any threat could not gain simple access. The Green Zone was the top prize for the insurgency to attack, but if a threat to the gate were even thought to happen, a barrage of gunfire would erupt to flatten any danger quickly and deadly.

Our convoy slowly and cautiously weaved through the entryway as we were waved forward while each truck was carefully inspected by coalition security specialists, watching our every move in great detail. There was no room for mistake entering the Green Zone, and it was perfectly clear as I presented my American military ID card to the gate's well-armed sentry. Once cleared to enter the Green Zone, the convoy's weapons were cleared as squad leaders carefully inspected each of the gun truck's weapon chambers. A misfire inside of a coalition compound was not a good thing in any way. Strict discipline or a possible court-martial was guaranteed to follow due to a weapon accidentally fired inside the gate. A misfire could easily be mistaken for an ambush or attack. Return fire at this point would be fierce and deadly within seconds.

The Green Zone resembled a small city within the enormous city of Baghdad. Dozens of Iraqi government buildings seemed to run on and on and on. Apartment complexes were spread throughout the area, and perfectly paved roads with beautiful palm trees decorated the main drag. Perfectly manicured lawns and bright-green gardens set between buildings reminding me of a typical American city, not a combat zone. People were walking in every direction, and cars were carelessly zooming about as our convoy shuffled forward to the hospital. It seemed everyone was casually talking on cell phones and wearing business suits. Women wore dresses with bright colors that to me were a welcomed sight. The Green Zone that morning was beginning to remind me of being back home in Indianapolis on a spring day.

The Corps' Hospital, or better known to coalition forces as the "CASH," was only six or seven blocks away from the Green Zone's main gate that we had just carefully entered. The hospital was huge, five or six stories tall. The main entrance to the CASH was constantly busy with foot traffic going in and out, doctors, patients, and military from all sorts of countries. A few soldiers who fell under the Eighty-Ninth Brigade were at the CASH, ranging from noncombat injuries, illness, or recently wounded during missions. While our senior officers went inside the hospital, I waited with the vehicles that were staged near the main doors of the CASH. I wanted to pick the brains of a few drivers who safely delivered us to the Green Zone that morning. Soon our company would be leading missions similar to today's convoy through Baghdad and beyond, and I wanted to be as knowledgeable as possible.

What was unusual within the safety of the Green Zone was large cement boxes painted bright yellow. The bulky concrete contraptions were at my guess twelve feet wide, ten feet long, and probably eight feet high. On each side of the strange boxes were what looked like small doorways but oddly without doors. On each side of the bizarre bright-yellow boxes had the words *duck and cover* in plain English, painted in bold black letters that could easily be seen for several blocks.

As the day dragged on and the Iraqi sun began to heat up to one hundred degrees, I asked the driver of my gun truck that led our convoy into the Green Zone why the bright-yellow cement boxes were at certain street corners.

"Those are duck and covers," the sergeant calmly explained. "Duck and covers are all over the place here."

"What is a duck and cover?" I asked after a slight hesitation.

"If shot at without any place to go…" the sergeant said as calm as he could possibly could. "Just jump into a duck and cover."

That explained the bright-yellow paint, easy to see.

"But we are in the Green Zone," I followed with. "Why jump for cover?"

"This place is not safe, sir," he said without expression. "And don't stand still in one place for over fifteen seconds at a time."

All of the *seasoned* soldiers of this convoy who were waiting at the trucks staged in front of the Green Zone CASH were doing just as the driver of my truck was doing, every fifteen seconds, taking a few steps in any direction. It was like clockwork. Every fifteen seconds, a few steps left, right, forward, or back. This kept a sniper from zeroing in on a possible target. Most soldiers from our convoy stood near their gun truck. This minimized you as a target. The truck was a little extra covered against an enemy sniper perched on a rooftop or darkened high-rise window.

I quickly adapted to the informal anti-sniper policy and would take a few steps every ten to fifteen seconds. It becomes natural after a few hours and becomes habit. I found myself moving consistently without really realizing I was doing it.

We had been briefed on the sniper threat that was a fairly new enemy tactic to Iraq while we were training at Fort Dix. Enemy snipers in Iraq were well trained and very accurate. Lately, these snipers were being trained to aim for throats, crotches, and faces. Al-Qaeda was producing training films to recruit snipers and to train snipers. Our intelligence had intercepted the training media and distributed it to us to show the danger.

The new threat to coalition in Iraq was brutal that attacked with fatal and disastrous consequences. Attacks were complex, well planned with results that left damage and carnage beyond belief. Iraqis that were caught working among coalition had recently been captured and tortured. Enemy captors filmed the Iraqi betrayer's final days while held in secret captivity. The hostages were starved, tortured, and eventually beheaded as the victims moaned and begged for mercy while their arms and legs were painfully bound by wire while gagged. Most videos showed close-up shots of the bruised and bloody face of the detainee as their captors waived a coalition ID badge stating they were allowed on American military bases. The images were horrific beyond imagine but were to show us just how vicious the enemy in Iraq was.

Our return trip to Camp Victory mirrored our earlier course that sunny Baghdad day, the highest level of security mixed with a dull, uneventful trip through western Baghdad. I continued to question the 180th leaders and soldiers of the convoy. In less than two weeks, they would be heading back to Kuwait, then return to the states and no longer available for valuable advice. I absorbed every bit of information I could gather from the 180th guys, and they did not hesitate to answer any and every question.

NCOs and junior enlisted of the 180th were great guys, but overall emotionless, it appeared. Rarely smiling or cracking jokes as our 152nd Infantry unit was very notorious for. But the 180th were ready to go home after proudly completing their one-year in Iraq. The Arizona guardsmen continued to serve their last few days in country with total professionalism and care. With just days remaining in Iraq, there was no room for mistake or tragedy. The freedom flight to Kuwait was within view, and getting home to family and friends was paramount.

After a year in Iraq, would our unit resemble the 180th? An emotionless and hardened bunch of combat veterans? Many of the 180th seemed to own the one-thousand-yard stare and were wore down and beaten from their combat tour in what was named "Operation Iraqi Freedom."

CHANGE OF MISSION

Fourth Platoon quickly prepared for duty at the mysterious and troubled Camp Ramadi, but we were not certain of the platoon's mission during our daily briefings and leadership meetings with the 180th leadership. Fourth was to assist with Ar Ramadi Iraqi Police, but that was merely all we knew. I had listened to soldiers of the 180th and what was going on at Camp Ramadi, but the details strangely seemed left out. We only knew Fourth was to pay the Iraqi Police once a month and check on the station once in a while just to make sure the police were okay, and that they were patrolling in the city limits without any problems.

To convoy to Ramadi meant traveling along one of the deadliest highways in Iraq, a deselect highway known as "Route Mobile." Route Mobile was a four-lane highway with a sandy median that basically ran east and west along the dangerous Euphrates River. Although Ramadi was only forty or forty-five miles away from Camp Liberty's west gate, the trek took two dangerous hours by military convoy, and this was a very, very boring drive along one of the world's most fatal thoroughfares known to mankind.

At the halfway point from Baghdad to Ramadi, there sat the Abu Ghraib Prison Complex. The prison was on the north side of the Route Mobile Iraqi highway, and this eerie structure could easily be seen from the roadside. The prison was difficult for me to even glance at; we were all fully aware of the disaster at the Abu Ghraib Prison prior to our arrival in Iraq. Fourth Platoon would be working closely with Ramadi's Iraqi policemen that included jail cells and prisoners, so 152nd leadership was determined that zero detainee abuse was to transpire in any way. We did not want to be associated with an international tragedy such as the Iraqi Abu Ghraib Prison disaster. Detainee abuse and atrocities were horrific in every way, so horrific that we were dedicated to have zero negative issues with abuse of Iraqi prisoners.

Just a few short months prior to our arrival in Iraq, several American soldiers were court-martialed and imprisoned for horrid detainee abuse that occurred at the Abu Ghraib Prison Complex. Seventeen soldiers that included the senior army officers were relieved of duty at the Abu Ghraib Prison. The army charged eleven soldiers with dereliction of duty that included Army Spec. Charles Graner. Graner was sentenced ten years in prison, and Army Pvt. 1st Cl. Lynndie England was sentenced to serve three years. Army Res. Brig. Gen. Janis Karpinski of the Eight-Hundredth Military Police Brigade was reduced in rank to colonel over the callous events that occurred at the Abu Ghraib Prison. Karpinski, with no prison supervision in her past, was in command of fifteen detention facilities throughout the Iraqi Theater during the international inmate catastrophe.

Along Route Mobile, farming communities and many small cities were strewn along the stretch of the dusty Iraqi highway between Baghdad and Ramadi. But the winding waterways and remote farming fields made it problematic to identify who was a true farmer or who could be plotting the next improvised explosive device or IED directed at unexpected convoys traveling through the flat desert region that ran along the historic waterway. During the summer months of 2006, IEDs were the most feared threat directed toward us, IEDs were silent killers who would strike with brutal, lethal consequences. Now Fourth Platoon, approximately twenty-five or twenty-seven guys, were placed in the area that had been a hotbed for deadly IED attacks. This had 152nd leadership worried and concerned.

Fourth quickly moved out to the isolated and desolate Camp Ramadi in the Al Anbar Province. The mission for Fourth was to join up with the Three-Hundredth Military Police who were currently mentoring and assisting Ramadi's Iraqi Police. The Iraqi Police were known as IPs and several stations were scattered throughout the city of Ramadi. The Three-Hundredth were an active duty military police unit with a home base at Fort Riley, Kansas. But we did not know much about the unit or their day-to-day mission or current duties in Ar Ramadi.

Within a few weeks into our tour of duty, I was able to make my first visit to Camp Ramadi by convoy. My assignment was to bring mail to Fourth Platoon, complete a health and welfare check on our 152nd guys at the camp, and inquire on just what their mission exactly was with the mysterious Iraqi policemen.

I found Camp Ramadi to be extremely dusty and seemed very secluded compared to the large coalition bases placed throughout the country of Iraq, a country that emulated the size of California. There was nothing to brag about regarding the living and working conditions for our 152nd guys at Camp Ramadi. The entire area seemed completely filthy and ragged. There were a few multilevel buildings in the middle of the camp, but most of the compound had rows and rows of temporary wooden buildings that were used for company headquarters and living quarters. Basically, the buildings were skimpy plywood shacks, hundreds of them.

Fourth Platoon's mission was to beef up numbers for the struggling Three-Hundredth who were assisting with daily IP operations. The Three-Hundredth were understrength and needed additional soldiers to support in their Iraqi Police advising and mentoring mission in the distressed city of Ramadi. Sgt. 1st Cl. Ronald Eller was our senior 152nd man on Camp Ramadi. Eller was from southwestern Indiana. He grew up with Amish neighbors and friends. Eller was rumored to have Amish ties, but we were not certain, and he would not confirm or deny.

Eller wore very thick glasses, and he possessed large spooky bug eyes that could hypnotize the best therapists in the business. Eller always bragged of his homemade blueberry winemaking skills and ability to grow corn in any environment. But Eller kept his personal life and Amish connections to himself.

I knew Eller had a first name initial consisting of J. And I had asked Eller if his first name was "Jebidiah," but the lifelong Hoosier did not appreciate the question and gave me a long dark look. He did not answer, and I did not ask again. The slinky senior NCO slowly turned around and strolled back to his wooden hut that was covered in a thick layer of dust from a recent sandstorm that had blasted the camp.

Camp Ramadi was a complete opposite of Liberty and Victory back in Baghdad. Any place in the Baghdad area was a decent place to be stationed in Iraq compared to Ramadi. Camps such as Liberty and Victory were well-known for their large dining facilities, paved roads, excellent food, USO concerts, and decent shows with comedians who were always performing at one of the two bases. Internet centers and gyms were outstanding to visit, while corps' palace stood out as the charm of the now ran coalition force's compound.

Camp Ramadi was a dust bowl that no one wanted to visit. And Fourth Platoon was there for the remainder of our yearlong combat tour.

But the good times did not last for the 152nd Infantry and its gravy duty at Camp Liberty in Baghdad. It took just under a month when our company received a change of mission order, along with a harsh change of location at filthy Camp Ramadi.

Camp Ramadi's Three-Hundredth Military Police were to rotate back to the states soon, and the 152nd Infantry was selected to replace the "Three-Hundredth Bulldogs" at the rugged and dusty Ramadi base. The Three-Hundredth were attached to the Army's historic First Armored Division's First Brigade for their one-year tour in Iraq, and the First Armored depended on the Three-Hundredth MPs to lead, guide, and mentor the IPs in the troubled city of Ramadi.

The First Armored Division is better known as "Old Ironsides" and renowned for its ferocious fighting ability during World War II's Operation Torch and the famed Italian Campaign. The First Division was named after the *USS Constitution Battleship*, "Old Ironsides," by the division's initial commander, Maj. Gen. Bruce Magruder. The two-star copied the ship's name as his division prepared for combat against the German Nazi Army. Magruder's "Old Ironsides" was the first armored division to engage in combat during World War II, and the First Armored was once again in the military spotlight in what would be known as the *surge* of Iraq.

Following the Operation Torch and the Italian Campaign, the First Armored had been widely used in every major military event since its flag was raised in 1940 at Fort Knox, Kentucky, to serve in World War II. The division was also called to serve during "Operation Desert Storm" during the Persian Gulf War in 1991 and was recently deployed to Afghanistan in 2011 to serve in "Operation Enduring Freedom."

Virginia senator John Warner first delivered the term "the surge" on notes taken during meetings with the Armed Services Committee regarding a buildup or expansion in Iraq. These notes scribbled on the senator's notepad demanded a sharp increase of personnel and equipment. A surge was the only option to the Iraqi problem according to Warner in order to curb the delicate, shaky situation currently in Iraq. A "surge was needed," the senior senator noted.

We knew the increase of violence in the Anbar Province needed to be settled in order to stabilize Iraq. Attacks against coalition forces, as well as noncombatants, were skyrocketing. The current lack of economic alternatives and high unemployment led to locals joining the insurgency for work. Due to looting and thousands of unaccountable munitions that had been built and stored throughout the area, IED material was plentiful and could easily be rigged and placed. Suicide bombings increased as well in Ramadi with casualties hitting all-time highs along with the insurgency hitting prominent locations such as marketplaces, religious sites, and highly populated neighborhoods. Locals were becoming frustrated and growing weary of the US involvement in Iraq and "Iraqi Freedom" during these distressed times in Anbar.

Al Anbar rested in the southwest corner of the feared Iraqi Triangle of Death. Catastrophic attacks were daily events for the

First Brigade that covered the province. Ramadi was a key city where suicide bombers usually met to plan and freely maneuver to their intended targets. IED threats were everywhere, major and alternative routes were very dangerous for coalition forces to travel in Anbar, and freedom of movement favored Al-Qaeda. Old Ironsides's First Brigade was tasked to change the threat in Anbar and needed the local police to help.

Despite the harsh and dangerous conditions at Camp Ramadi, I was glad to once again serve under the First Armored Division. In January of 1996, I was assigned to the division in northeast Bosnia. Old Ironsides was the command element of Task Force Eagle based at Tuzla Air Base, a multinational effort intended to maintain peace in the troubled Yugoslavian region.

Ramadi was located in a deep solid Sunni area, a Sunni location that completely idolized the former Iraqi leader, Saddam Hussain. Although Saddam was from the small town of Takrit, approximately seventy miles to the north of Ar Ramadi, he was adored by the people in the Al Anbar Province. The Anbar Sunnis lived very well during the Saddam regime with luxury apartment complexes, running water, electricity, and a fantastic highway system. But the Saddam trial was coming to a close when our infantry company made the move to Camp Ramadi as we prepared to work in the community with the Iraqi Police. We were unsure of how the community would react to the final outcome of the trial that drew international attention.

We were mindful that Iraq's Camp Ramadi was patented "Crazy Ramadi," and with the international news of the upcoming execution for Saddam, we were unsure of what reaction could erupt. The entire province that surrounded Ramadi was also acknowledged by coalition intelligence to be an insurgent stronghold, freely able to move and operate. The insurgency unquestionably had the upper hand, and intel reports confirmed we were in the hot spot of danger in the country.

After I arrived at Camp Ramadi, I found that the Three-Hundredth was a very troubled unit both internally and externally. The unit had a pair of commanders recently relieved or better known as fired. Morale was horrible and at an all-time low with the Three-Hundredth Military Police Company. I arrived with the company's advance party, nine of us in total. Prior to the remaining one hundred-plus 152nd soldiers arriving, I needed to ensure that living and working quarters were lined up and in order.

I could not locate the Three-Hundredth commander, but I did bump into the unit's first sergeant and operations sergeant. The pair of MPs informed me that the unit was leaving the country with or without formal orders. The first sergeant was not going to show the advance party the ropes, assist with living arrangements, or offer the usual—and theater required—proper relief in place or RIP procedure. They were just going to leave and did not care much about theater formalities or procedures. Being the senior man on Camp Ramadi for the 152nd, I requested a tour of Camp Ramadi to see where the medic station was, location of brigade headquarters, and so on. I was told to "use my boots." So I did. I walked the entire dusty, dirty camp by foot as Three-Hundredth's vehicles sat in the motor pool.

Three months prior to my arrival at Camp Ramadi, a pair of Three-Hundredth soldiers were injured in an attack at a nearby police station. The Three-Hundredth MPs then decided to quit. This mission to assist in the IP effort was no longer their job, and this mission was not what they were trained to do. They just quit. Their vehicles were parked, equipment was perfectly laid out and cleaned for inspection to hand over to someone else, anyone else, and they were leaving the country. Once meeting one of the MP's lieutenants, his first words to me were, "You are the 152nd executive officer? Good, sign for these vehicles and equipment so we can leave!" And he meant exactly what he said. They were leaving. I am not sure where they were going to go, but they were definitely set on leaving Camp Ramadi and leave quickly.

Within the next few days of being at Camp Ramadi, while awaiting the 152nd "main body" to arrive with the company supply sergeant and commander to properly account and sign for the property, I had wished that the Three-Hundredth had left as they had promised. The Three-Hundredth wanted to leave and leave right away but could not leave without property and material signed over to the incoming 152nd company commander. We knew this, they knew this, and the Three-Hundredth took their frustrations out on us, the 152nd advance party. My time with the advance party arriving was definitely the worse eight days of my military career to be as clear and frank as possible.

I was somehow able to find out our new mission was to work, live, supply, and lead the Iraqi police assigned to the several police stations in the Ramadi area. The key emphasis was recruiting and training additional police for the main police station located in central Ramadi, as well as assisting the smaller stations in the area. Secondary was construction of a few more police stations in Ar Ramadi. The Ready First Brigade was strongly focused on the police stations to bring security to the region and not fail, but the stagnant Three-Hundredth was in their way.

We were also working with civilian contractors who were implementation police liaison officers, better known to us as IPLOs. The IPLOs were in Iraq to work closely with the Iraqi Police and fine-tune their policing skills. Much like our unit, the IPLOs were mentors for the IPs. IPLO mentoring and training was very basic, simple skills such as handcuffing, vehicle patrols, paperwork, prisoner accountability, weapon qualification, and weapon use.

The Ramadi IPLOs lived well at Camp Ramadi. The contractors had their own secluded area to live and work out of what was just a few miles from of our headquarters area, but their housing and working area was more of a campground. The IPLOs owned a cluster of seven or eight wooden shacks that was the furthest spot on camp from the main base in the south sector of Camp Ramadi. But the IPLOs had not intermingled with the local IPs for several weeks due to the fact they needed to be escorted by the American army team assigned to police stations. The Three-Hundredth did not run missions to stations, so the IPLOs did not go. But the lax times were about to change for the Ramadi IPLOs. We were eager to get to the stations and bring the IPLOs with us. The IPLOs were becoming board with daily cookouts and watching movies at night. These guys were ready to get back to the stations and work with the new 152nd Infantry guys.

I first met the IPLO team in secrecy. The Three-Hundredth did not want us to know about or meet the civilians who were to work with us in Ar Ramadi. On my third day at Ramadi, I walked with two other 152nd soldiers to the IPLO neighborhood and did a quick meet and greet. The IPLOs were great guys, former or retired police officers under government contract in Iraq. When I arrived, music was blaring from a makeshift courtyard in the middle of their wooden shack metropolis, and a charcoal grill was fired up with several seasoned steaks simmering. Also on the grill were loads of fresh vegetables with a pile of baked potatoes.

"We knew you would be here soon." Smiled the IPLO station chief, Sam Garritt, who went by the name "Grit" as he tended the grill. "Stay for lunch!" Grit demanded as he continued to jab the perfectly seasoned steaks with a large fork. A quick blast of desert wind left a faint dusting of sand that covered the steaks and vegetables, but Grit didn't bother the minor inconvenience and continued to monitor the grilling. This was just another day in Ramadi. Just another fine coat of sand on your dinner. That's all, just another dusty, hot day in the desert.

The Ramadi IPLO team was aware that a change was quickly in work from the Ready First leadership. The plan from brigade was to remove the Three-Hundredth and replace with an infantry unit to run the Iraqi Police station mission in Ar Ramadi. The IPLO crew was thrilled to hear of the change and was eager to return to police stations once the Three-Hundredth had officially left Ramadi.

The Three-Hundredth hung around Camp Ramadi for a week or so after the remaining 152nd soldiers arrived, but the shunned MPs did very little for our unit or assist in the transfer. I remembered the solid, never-break rule from the army's Warrior Ethos script, "I will never quit." So much for that with the Three-Hundredth Military Police's so-called "Bulldogs." Every unit on Camp Ramadi hated this unit with a pure passion.

The Three-Hundredth were referred to as "the unit we will not mention by name" by senior Camp Ramadi leadership. It was simply disgusting to even stand near members of this pathetic unit and its leadership. Each time I heard the phrase, "The unit we will not mention by name," the verbiage made me cringe as an American soldier, but the embarrassing phrase for the Three-Hundredth was well deserved.

MARC'S MECHANICS

Each evening, leadership from the 152nd met to discuss how the handover was going, and the broken vehicle situation was the most vital point to discuss. Henton at times found me laboring in the dusty 152nd motor pool, wrench in hand and working side-by-side with our junior enlisted mechanics. The motor pool was near the company area, across the street from our headquarters shack. To the east of the motor pool was Camp Ramadi's "signal hill" that had a dozen or so military antennas and a few satellite dishes on its peak. The motor pool sat in the cool shade of signal hill in the morning and was a great place to sit atop in the evening as the sun disappeared into the horizon of the Iraqi desert.

Our top priority at Camp Ramadi was the forty vehicles that were handed over to our 152nd mechanics from the Three-Hundredth. Shockingly, only eight of the unit's forty gun trucks were considered operational. We also had six armored security vehicles in our inventory, better known as ASVs. The ASVs were larger and safer than the Hummer and could transport five troops that included the gunner in the top hatch.

The deadlined trucks were a huge problem for our mission. We simply could not run missions with 80 percent of our vehicles broke and sitting in the motor pool, and the task to fix the trucks fell upon our maintenance team led by Sgt. 1st Cl. Marc Laddy. Marc had just over eighteen years of both active duty and National Guard experience, all as an Army mechanic. Marc was with our company during hurricane relief efforts in Mississippi and Louisiana following Hurricane Katrina's destruction just a year prior to our company's arrival to Iraq. His knowledge and leadership kept our company mobile during the hurricane relief. Now he was tasked to do the same in Ramadi.

As soon as our 152nd mechanics arrived at Camp Ramadi, Marc and his wrench team quickly went to work on the broken vehicles. It did not take long to fix the vehicle dilemma. Within ten days, the dead-lined vehicle count dropped to a mere six. Henton was overly impressed with the miraculous change in downed versus operational vehicles. Our unit rebounded from questioning the fact of not running missions to being mission ready in record time. Thanks to our mechanics.

Our Ready First leadership was also impressed with Laddy and the 152nd mechanics. Our brigade at Camp Ramadi was assured that the Three-Hundredth did not want operational trucks to run missions with. Inoperable trucks meant no missions.

The Ready First was mesmerized and quickly saw us as a vital asset for the perilous IP mission.

READY FIRST

The First Armored Division's First Brigade commander was Col. Sean MacFarland, and the colonel's brigade was affectionately known as the "Ready First." MacFarland's brigade was tasked to return the troubled province's fight back to the coalition force's favor, and the colonel was always on the front line of the fight for Ramadi. The colonel urgently needed to relieve the absconding Three-Hundredth and bring in a combat arms unit to run the police stations as the surge was beginning to mature. And Colonel MacFarland was thrilled to hear that the 152nd Infantry "Cyclones" were now on ground and ready to run missions.

MacFarland was a slender man, standing at just under six feet. His positive personality was infectious, and he was willing to meet and shake the hand of any nearby soldier, always making eye contact. The colonel could remember everyone's name, had a warm and welcoming smile, but he always kept his right palm resting on his Beretta pistol secured to his pistol belt.

Colonel MacFarland was on a short list to be selected to brigadier general, and victory in Anbar Province would undoubtedly seal the deal for the promotion.

Colonel MacFarland's deputy commanding officer was Lt. Col. Jim Lechner, his DCO. We would work closely with Lechner; he was tasked by MacFarland to oversee the Ramadi police stations and bring nothing but success. Colonel MacFarland also had in his war chest a young Marine Corps officer who was assigned as his police station implementation officer, Maj. Teddy Gates. Major Gates was in charge of Iraqi Police recruiting and training in the greater Ramadi area. The brigade commander knew that without proper police recruiting combined with solid training, his mission would result in pure failure.

Major Gates also reported to Maj. Gen. Joseph Peterson who was in command of training the Iraqi Police throughout Iraq.

We began our tenure at Camp Ramadi by conducting interviews and testing for future Iraqi policemen on the camp that included a scan of the recruit's eyeballs. The eye scan is much like a fingerprint; no two are the same. A quick physical fitness test that consisted of a few dozen sit-ups followed by several correct pushups was all it took. Some education was required to include a decent knowledge of reading and writing of the Iraqi language. Once the candidate finished the academy, he would be assigned to a station as an official Iraqi policeman.

We did have a problem with one recruit. I was summoned to the testing area one morning and to bring one set of handcuffs. Following a renal eye scan of a police recruit, the scan revealed that the candidate was wanted for murder against coalition forces in 2005. Shortly after the grim discovery, I and a team of four 152nd soldiers were ordered to transport the suspect to the Camp Ramadi Detention Center. My instruction to the detail was not to have the suspected recruit dragged out of the training building. The handover to my Humvee was to be swift and without incident. I did not want a scene in front of the other IP recruits. The sought Iraqi was requested to step outside to assist with bringing food into the cafeteria. I had Staff Sergeant Jason Brawn waiting outside to handcuff the suspect for transport to the detention center. The plan and execution worked perfectly. We did not want to cause a scene or have the other hundred or so recruits to think they also could be dragged out and taken away in handcuffs. We never saw the alleged Iraqi murderer again.

I later briefed Lieutenant Colonel Lechner of the incident, and our detail was given a well done by the DCO.

Lieutenant Colonel Lechner was strikingly different from his commanding officer, the easygoing Colonel MacFarland. The DCO was once assigned to the spectacle of the military, the US Army's Seventy-Fifth Ranger Brigade. The hard-nosed Lechner stood only at five foot five, was very stalky, and incredibly driven.

MacFarland recognized that Lechner was a perfect fit for the Al Anbar mission that at times seemed the impossible task. The DCO showed no fear and was known to valiantly walk down the city streets of Ar Ramadi, marching side by side with his Iraqi military and police equals. Lechner was also on a one-man mission, it seemed, to find an invisible enemy artillery piece that was causing havoc, as well as casualties, on Camp Ramadi. The DCO believed the piece was buried or well concealed on the southwest side of Ar Ramadi. If the piece was underground, it was hidden by a truck or something large that could be moved quickly. The weapon was quickly uncovered and fired toward Camp Ramadi, then covered back up without detection. We were told Navy SEALs eventually located the artillery piece that was causing the trouble, and the veiled threat disappeared. But we did not hear details of the find; the SEALs worked quietly and did not expect nor want praise. Being praised or honored was not the Navy SEAL's way.

Major Gates enjoyed being with our teams at the police stations and in the recruiting offices. The boyish-looking marine would spend twelve to fourteen hours a day off the base closely interacting with his Iraqi colleagues, enjoying chai tea in the mornings and a plate of lamb in the evening with police station leadership. He would not discuss the Three-Hundredth MPs that had recently departed Camp Ramadi, but I am sure Major Gates did not appreciate their lack of effort in the coalition's undertaking in Al Anbar and looked to us to turn tables quickly in Ar Ramadi. And we were fated to provide the winning hand to Gates and the brigade leadership.

Prior to our arrival at Camp Ramadi, Major Gates and Colonel MacFarland requested seven senior noncommissioned officers and officers of the Three-Hundredth be relieved of duty. The Three-Hundredth Bulldogs' higher command—the Ninety-Second, based at Camp Liberty—would only relieve the company commander. The company commander was overall responsible for all right or wrong under his command, and he was removed. The First Armored senior leadership was furious that the sole Three-Hundredth soldier to be removed was the company commander. The First wanted all seven gone, but that did not happen. The MPs fell under the brigade's operational control but not their direct command.

With little or nothing changed following the removal of the Three-Hundredth company commander, the First Armored could only sit and wait until the shameful Three-Hundredth was ready to move back to Kuwait and eventually be replaced with a new unit. Morale and recruiting with the Ramadi IPs dove to drastic levels, and the insurgency continued to grow in Anbar.

The Three-Hundredth remained in hiding as the First Armored Brigade and its several attached supporting units ran dangerous missions day by day in the province without police assistance. The stagnant Bulldogs could not be found, and Ready First wrote the military police unit off as useless.

The proud Ready First was equipped with seventy-three monstrous M1 Abrams tanks and eighty-four Bradley Infantry Fighting Vehicles that dominated the city of Ar Ramadi. The Bradleys were smaller than the Abrams tank yet powerful war machines, quicker, and much more agile than the mighty Abrams. But with this overall firepower, the First Brigade needed the streets and neighborhoods safe and secure as their armored vehicles patrolled neighborhoods and led convoys throughout the region. The critical Iraqi police stations were desperately needed to secure and protect the roads, bridges, waterways, and neighborhoods. Patrolling and freedom of coalition movement were vital to Colonel MacFarland, and the brigade's senior leadership could not wait to see the Three-Hundredth leave. Ready First needed a combat arms unit to work with the Iraqi Police and pressured the Eighty-Ninth to replace the ghost Three-Hundredth Military Police Company with a unit that would run the police stations and build them up to complete the Anbar Awakening mission. The Eighty-Ninth gave them us, Alpha Company of the 152nd Infantry.

As the Three-Hundredth stayed in hiding somewhere on Camp Ramadi, the operation's cell did have a few soldiers posted in the headquarters shack, but the company's one hundred or so soldiers were nowhere to be found on the camp. The Three-Hundredth were well-known as the black eye of Camp Ramadi. Outhouses near the company area had plenty of creative poems scribbled in them, stating how Ready First units felt of the Three-Hundredth: "300, Go Home!" "Hey Bulldogs, wish you weren't here!" "Thank you, ladies of the 300th…we won't tell your husbands!" The Three-Hundredth did have female soldiers, ten or twelve from what I had been told. And the pisshouse poet's comments about them were my favorite to read, as well as the Chuck Norris posts of his greatness and might.

Chuck Norris recently visited Camp Ramadi during a USO tour of Iraq. He was always eager to shake the hand of every soldier and wish them luck. Norris' greatness was plastered in every outhouse. I do not know exactly why, but outhouses were a favorite for outhouse lyricists.

Shortly after the Three-Hundredth finally left Iraq, we officially began our assigned mission with the Ar Ramadi Iraqi Police. Our much-anticipated assignment involved eight police stations, manned with just over 1,500 policemen. We basically learned the IP mission on our own with zero assistance from the Three-Hundredth. But we quickly adapted to the Iraqi Police tasking.

Colonel MacFarland was quick to personally bring his Ready First leadership to our new 152nd company area once the final Three-Hundredth soldier had left Camp Ramadi. He brought Major Gates and Lt. Colonel Lechner along with his trusted brigade sergeant major. It was an honor to meet Jim Lechner, who bravely served in Somalia. During the 1993 Battle of Mogadishu, Lechner was deployed as the executive officer and fire direction officer for the Army Rangers in Somalia. He would eventually be seriously wounded during the tragic battle that inspired the book "Blackhawk Down."

We were told that after the Three-Hundredth departed Ramadi, they had a huge and luxurious awards ceremony at the main side of TQ. Bronze Star Medals, Commendation Medals and certificates of appreciation were distributed to all of the members of the Three-Hundredth just a few days prior to the unit's departure from Iraq.

The first IP station that I was able to visit was Ar Ramadi's main police station. The main station was located in the heart of Ar Ramadi. Apartment buildings surrounded its perimeter and a small market was located to the south of the complex. The main station was once a campground for Iraqi boys, similar to Boy Scout campgrounds back in the states. But the former camp for boys was now the critical IP station. The station had a huge banquet room, two courtyards, several rows of jail cells, and a large variety of living quarters for staff.

My initial visit to the main Ramadi Police Station was very uneventful, just meeting a few of the station's leadership, and I was able to check out what the station was equipped with. They recognized we were new in Ramadi, and we were at times tested by the not so reluctant Iraqis at the station. Most IPs wanted gifts or favors. But we wanted friendship, trust, and loyalty.

Each of the police stations included jails with policemen trained in the detention field and detainee handling. And with recent prison-related disasters in the country, I continued to stress to our soldiers to not violate the rules of war, specifically rules regarding prisoners of war and handling detainees. Basically, my instructions were to be humane. I stressed what my former brigade commander, and later Army National Guard Major General Ivan Denton, would say of doing the right thing, "Don't do anything you wouldn't want your mother to see." This was solid advice from a fantastic leader.

The Iraqi police mission was simple according to the First Armored Brigade that we were now "operationally" attached to; make the Iraqi Police successful in every way. In turn, the IPs will govern the area, along the side of the Iraqi Army, and peace will be brought back to the troubled region. Too easy, right?

NUMBERS AND EXTENSIONS

Our infantry unit arrived in Iraq just before the surge. Troop strength shot up to 165,000 in direct support of Operation Iraqi Freedom late 2006, and that number was very certain to rise. But the surge was not really a surge, as in a huge wave of new units to support the coalition effort. Many of the units on ground were what was called "involuntarily extended." Typically, unit tours were twelve-months long, give or take a few weeks. Leaving Iraq depended on how smooth the replacement unit's arrival went and how much time was spent in Kuwait preparing to move north to Iraq. But several units in Iraq were given an extension of five to six additional months, usually ordered to remain in the same location, same job, and same command structure.

Any unit with orders to serve in Iraq meant that a dull and boring process must be completed in Kuwait. Units were required to spend twelve to twenty days in Kuwait at one of its several military bases to acclimatize to the fierce desert heat, participate in a few required classes, and provided a last-chance opportunity to test-fire all weapons prior to departing to the Iraqi combat zone. I knew something big was about to happen while we were in Kuwait. The small remote bases were packed to the max with units preparing to move north to Iraq. We did not know of the surge or what was really going on in Iraq at that point. I just knew something big was going on, and we were going to be in the middle of it.

While our company was in Kuwait and just shy of one week waiting to push north to Baghdad, the First Cavalry Brigade arrived. The cav was moving through Kuwait in record speed. The cav *bumped* us from processing and moving, as well as several other units waiting to move north. Our commander took this personal and didn't like the fact we were to be delayed by the cav's stampede through Kuwait. But we were against the army's prized First Cavalry, and I tried my best to ease Henton's mind that the First Cav was too powerful to fight. The cav's commander was handed priority processing for his regiment, and he was going to get it.

"We are just an Army National Guard company," I stressed. "They are the active duty First Cavalry."

Henton eventually conceded and could only watch as the cav that arrived weeks after us was scuttled north in the matter of a few days.

As far as the existing units that were still in Iraq, many were notified of the extension within a few months of their proposed departure from theater, and some were notified of the extension within only a few weeks of their scheduled departure from the Iraqi theater. What a depressor for units packed and ready to get out of Iraq and return to their wives, families, college classes, and a normal life outside of Iraq and a harsh combat zone. It was a huge, huge morale buster for these selected units ordered to stay. Many of the commands designated for extension knew it could happen. Most commanders personally addressed their soldiers with the possibility of staying a few extra months in theater, and nothing could be done. Basically be prepared and plan for an extension. It seemed that if you had four or less months remaining, brace yourself for a longer stay in Iraq and keep chugging along with a smile. Not much more could be done.

One unit selected to stay was the Stryker Infantry Brigade serving in the war-tattered west Baghdad area. The brigade had its containers packed, sealed up, and most of the brigade's equipment was on its way home. When the order formally hit, the Stryker Brigade's cargo ships were ordered to return the unit's shipping containers to Iraq. Although packed and halfway home, the Stryker Brigade was ordered to stay in Iraq and return to the fight.

The Stryker Brigade, known as the "Artic Wolves," already had three hundred of its soldier's home in Alaska, preparing for the main body's triumphant return. Another three hundred soldiers were in Kuwait, ready to board flights back to the US. But ground commander, Gen. William Casey, was ordered by Secretary of Defense Donald Rumsfeld to keep the Artic Wolves of 3,800 soldiers in Baghdad as coalition forces' safety became top priority. General Casey became desperate with trouble in Iraq, and the war was quickly spinning out of control.

Casey didn't plan to replace the Artic Wolves in Western Baghdad, desiring a drawdown. But the secretary of defense ordered the ground commander to return the brigade to Iraq and continue their combat tour. Western Baghdad was in disarray and deadly. Casey looked like a fool.

Although the four-star was ordered to halt the Artic Wolves' departure from theater, General Casey continued to assure the White House that "Iraq was way ahead" regarding progress in July of 2006, and that the country's transition to Iraqi control was guaranteed within eighteen months minus the troubled Al Anbar Province.

But only a few months later, the update did not hold true for the fractured four-star general, and this alarmed President George W. Bush. Casey had detailed to President Bush and key civilian leaders that 295,000 Iraqi security forces were fully trained and serving in Iraq with coalition forces. Casey added that as soon as December of 2006, over 330,000 Iraqi security forces would be trained and on duty. But enemy attacks against coalition increased, and the insurgency was claiming victory as future plans for Americans leaving Iraq became public. Casey continued to say the situation was fine and on track in Iraq, but the White House and Pentagon were not listening to the commanding general's planning any longer.

Why did General Casey retain a regiment while requesting drawdown?

The surge effort was redirected from Gen. Tommy Franks's original strategy during spring of 2003. General Franks, then commander of Central Command, prepped and planned for a quick and furious sweep through Baghdad and beyond nearly four years prior to the loss of control in 2006. But Operation Iraqi Freedom was something different from Franks's planning during Operation Desert Shield in 1990 and 1991 of routing the Iraqi Army from Kuwait brought on by a powerful air blitz followed by a four-day devastating ground attack. Franks's design delivered a magnificent victory over Saddam Hussain's battered military in 1991. But this was fifteen years earlier to the surge. And Casey was in charge of the troubled and failing Iraq campaign.

As Franks sat in his CentCom office in central Saudi Arabia on the nineteenth of March 2003, ready to brief President Bush, Secretary of Defense Rumsfeld, and Secretary of State Condoleezza Rice, his reply to the president was, "We are well prepared for this attack." And he was. American Forces, combined with British and Australian Forces, marched north with great success, a sweeping stride that awed critics and dazzled envious commanders.

All this was accomplished with much less than what Gen. H. Norman Schwarzkopf had assembled during the 1990–'91 Gulf War in which Franks was a brigadier general in charge of planning. Schwarzkopf and Franks accomplished the 1991 victory with 560,000 troops, forming an incredible amount of fourteen coalition divisions. Franks, spending his early general-grade rank with the First Cavalry, was well-praised for his planning and coordination during the 1991 Gulf War. And he was not about to show anything different of his maneuver skills during the '03 sweep through Baghdad.

But Franks and Schwarzkopf were different. As a career infantryman, Schwarzkopf came from a military family, and he was raised in New York with a father, an army colonel, serving in Iraq as an advisor ironically. Franks grew up in the small town of Wynnewood, Oklahoma, and his hardworking family had little during his childhood and upbringing.

Franks's 2003 plan was clear, move swift, fast, speedy, and flexible with a very destructive objective—move and destroy. Coalition forces toppled the Saddam military faster than the media could relay information. Franks was pleased, and the world was fascinated by his brilliant and well-thought-out plan and maneuver mind.

My thought, as an infantry officer, is the cavalry better at large maneuvering than infantry? Or is it the man? Franks versus Schwarzkopf.

But the war at hand would change quickly in just a few short years. President Bush would call an end to combat operations early 2006. It was a surprise to many, and it seemed as if the world had paused for a deep breath as the smoke slowly cleared. But the war would change to "this is an Iraqi problem, we need an Iraqi solution." I became sick of hearing this overused quote. Why not say, "Sure, we leveled their country, now let's tell them to fix it." Coalition forces were now directing efforts to rebuild the Iraqi Army and Iraqi Police or better known as the country's security forces. But the insurgency had other plans and would not go away easily. Similar to World War II's Battle of the Bulge, the enemy regrouped for a fierce and deadly and bloody counterattack.

Soldiers were needed to complete this gigantic unrealistic task that was christened "the surge" by planners in Washington. This massive task included mobilizing and moving five additional combat brigades into Iraq. Five additional brigades were given the thumbs up by President Bush, but additional support personnel were needed to assist the additional brigades. Additional money, supplies, and housing were quickly needed to be pushed into the country. But additional troops and supplies were something current ground commander General Casey was strongly against. The White House and Joint Chiefs were wanting more troops on ground to secure the country; Casey was thinking of drawdown with his signature leave-to-win strategy. Casey was touting stability and promising withdrawal to the Iraqi minister of defense. But the reduction of troops was not going to happen demanded leaders in Washington.

Coalition forces had a total of sixty-nine US bases throughout Iraq in 2006, but Casey's immediate plan was to reduce that number by a ridiculous 84 percent, leaving only eleven bases. "This will happen," the general was quoted. Hearing of the general's statement, US Secretary of State Rice immediately departed DC and traveled to Iraq with a team of forty-eight staffers to speak directly with General Casey at his Iraqi headquarters within the walls of the Green Zone. Rice was becoming irritated with lack of control in Iraq and was quoted that Casey "didn't have a strategy," and she wanted face time with the commander.

Casey fumed of the upcoming Rice visit with a very large entourage in tow, stating "that is a paltry number." At this point of the war and crisis, Casey did not want to be pushed or intimidated by anyone, specifically a woman. "Additional forces will only have a temporary effect," Casey added.

Rice had recently commented that overall progress in Iraq was sliding *sideways*, and that Baghdad was evolving into *mob rule*. She was not pleased with the current conditions in Iraq, and all attention and blame were directed at the easily irritated General Casey who preferred to lead from the safety of his headquarters.

As Rice was preparing for the trip to Iraq, President Bush hinted of his displeasure with Casey during a press briefing at the White House. Casey kept hinting of his dreadful plan of rapid withdrawal into another year as attacks against coalition forces continued to sharply rise while the mission was falling apart in Iraq. That's when the president stated he was not interested in "ideas that would lead to defeat. I reject those ideas." A change of direction in Iraq was desperately needed by the White House.

Casey's plans for winning by timetable had not worked in the past, but the general somehow wanted another try at it. Operation "Together Forward" followed by "Together Forward Part 2" failed miserably, and Casey's "Together Forward Part 3" was not going to be allowed by Washington. Deadly insurgent attacks increased by the day, Americans were being crippled and killed by the dozens, and coalition forces had quickly lost the upper hand. Operation Iraqi Freedom's future was quickly slipping away.

Something different needed to be implemented during the final months of 2006 in place of another Casey drawdown proposal. Troop increases were needed to strengthen the coalition effort in certain regions of Iraq. Forces were added mainly in Baghdad and the Al Anbar Province that edged the border of Syria. Troop levels were also beefed up in Balad and Tikrit, both located in northern Iraq. Recruiting additional Iraqi policemen, standing additional police stations, and hiring additional Iraqi Army recruits were to aid in the surge.

I did not feel there needed to be additional soldiers brought into Iraq for a *surge*, but coalition leaders instead needed better management of its existing soldiers, marines, and airmen already placed in Iraq. There were too many Forward Operation Bases or FOBs that housed far too many troops doing meaningless or pathetic jobs, assistant purchaser of wood products, base temporary housing office staff, security detail watching sandbag stacking…you name it, there was an office for it, too many staffing it, and each had their own SUV, trailer to live in, and big office with couches and phones, of course, with Internet, and with stacks and stacks of water bottles everywhere. All this while a handful of grunts or a squad manned a checkpoint twenty-four hours a day, seven days a week on a lonely highway in the desert. These soldiers manning remote outposts were lucky to receive mail once a week, enjoy one hot meal each week, and lived with very little comfort creatures such as basic power. And when the grunts would return to a base, they would be ticketed by a sergeant major for parking vehicles too close to a doorway, specifically while attempting to load the next month's food supply for their remote, dangerous, and highly targeted checkpoint. At Camp Victory, home of the corps headquarters, sergeant majors were known to give speeding tickets to bicyclers or the scolding of soldiers for walking the wrong way around Z Lake by a corps staff member who really didn't even have a meaningful job.

President Bush knew an alternative, different approach was needed in Iraq. An alarming fifty to seventy-five American soldiers were being killed each month during the summer months of 2006, and millions of American tax dollars were being aimlessly spent on the war effort. And worse, there was no proof of the president's "weapons of mass destruction" theory. The press was simply destroying President Bush, and his poll numbers were sinking quickly. The president then went to his professionals for an answer. However, he went to too many professionals for answers. This was a trait that the president was well known to possess, one that truly needed an authoritarian-style decision in place of a vote.

The president wanted the incoming secretary of defense Robert Gates to "have time to evaluate the (Iraq) situation" as he began to settle in at his new position at The Pentagon. President Bush also ordered his Joints Chiefs to present a new approach for victory in Iraq that did not involve drawdowns. The president also appointed "the council of colonels" that included then Col. H. R. McMaster to brainstorm "what to do for victory in Iraq."

President Bush also had self-described Middle East expert Derek Harvey advise him of several key points that were immediately troubling Iraq and the war effort. The president was informed that $1 million in US funding per month was being pumped into the Ar Ramadi area from neighboring country of Syria; this was feeding and fueling the insurgency. "Anbar was the true problem at hand," according to Harvey, and fixing Ar Ramadi was "vital in order to stabilize Iraq."

President Bush was shocked with the facts of the briefing.

With Harvey's input, the retired army general Jack Keane was very open regarding Iraq's situation with President Bush, the Joint Chiefs, and the newly appointed secretary of defense. Keane's stern answer was that the president needed a much larger concentration of coalition forces in Iraq and in place quickly before the situation became worse. These additional forces needed to "live with and among the Iraqi security forces and people," Keane stated. This effort would separate the insurgency from the locals and provide instant stability in Iraq, delivering a quick victory.

The president sat motionless but knew what was needed. He needed "the surge."

General Keane served in an advisory role during the early management of the Iraq War for President Bush, and no longer wearing the uniform gave him freedom to freely advise without the worry of what senior leaders thought. This new ability to speak openly pleased Keane, and the retired four-star savored his key position within the White House.

Keane suggested that thirty thousand troops were needed to be immediately deployed to Iraq to kick off "the surge" while doubling Iraqi security forces to a whopping six hundred thousand army and policemen. Perhaps Keane's master's degree in philosophy from Western Kentucky University assisted the retired general in his advisement of the president. The president was desperately seeking solid advice and guidance in troubled Iraq that he had termed "mission complete" a year earlier. But now, he could only watch as the country was spiraling away into a dark and ugly abyss.

Another advisor to the president was the deputy national security advisor to Iraq Megan O'Sullivan. The deputy was summoned to the White House, and she provided a plan that also stressed that the president "double down" Iraqi security forces. O'Sullivan echoed Keane's thirty thousand additional troops to be thrusted into the fight in the troubled Iraq War effort. O'Sullivan was not fond of General Casey's "drawdown dreaming" in Iraq, and that the current ground commander's effort was "a complete failure," and she added the current plan "wasn't working at all."

Although she had no military experience, O'Sullivan had a clear view of Iraq and its potential for success with new direction. The young, very direct redhead delivered solid ideas and topics to President Bush during numerous meetings in the Oval Office but insisted that the current commanding general was not to be included in the planning or conservation of the increase of troops. Her department knew too well that General Casey was against additional troops. President Bush had O'Sullivan's full attention and was very impressed with the deputy's ideas and thoughts.

With Keane and O'Sullivan's advice and insight, President Bush ordered the deployment of 210,000 additional troops to Iraq on January 10, and the surge was in full force.

This was at our main Ramadi Police Station after a few rounds were fired into the complex. We were always fired at while visiting our police stations. The enemy hated us.

This is in our operations shack, that had very large maps of Ramadi. A platoon is briefed prior to a mission in Ramadi.

PAYDAY—payday was the first of every month for the Iraqi Police. We did not want to be short on cash or forget to pay an "IP". We paid in cash, "Dinar" was the Iraqi currency.

A 152 Soldier sits on his gun truck prior to a mission. Many of our gunners were very young, 19 and 20 year-olds.

"TQ just before leaving Iraq", In front of the
buildings we lived and worked out of.

At the Husaybah Police Station was a large hookah pipe,
usually filled with dried apples mixed with tobacco. I
have never smoked, but the taste was really good.

This is the Husaybah Police station with one of the two assistant chiefs standing next to one of the Marines that worked with us. The station belonged to a local tribal leader that was very wealthy. The house was more of a palace and very beautiful.

This is a tribal warrior from Northern Anbar that assisted in the mission known as "Operation Buttercup" in Tameem. These warriors were not Iraqi Police, but fought against the Insurgency and had a deep hatred toward them.

THE WILD WEST

Prior to being tasked to serve on the council of colonels, McMaster served as commander the Third Armored Cavalry Regiment located in Tal Afar, Iraq, early 2005, and his regiment stayed through the winter of 2006. Tal Afar was located in the district of the Nineveh Governorate of northwestern Iraq, and McMaster knew that this was an area that was completely infested by the insurgency as his regiment arrived. The region had a civilian population at just over two hundred thousand, and this land was very difficult to manage because Tal Afar was rich in sectarian divisions.

McMaster adored his Third "Brave Rifles" Regiment and his command position. The Third Mounted Riflemen was authorized by an Act of Congress on the first of December 1845 and had been called to duty dating back to the Indian Wars and Mexican-American War. The glamorous third was once again called up for deployment and was now in McMaster's hands in a very tough spot.

Demographically, Tal Afar is very isolated from major populated areas of Iraq. The region has a strong Iraqi Turkmen population, and McMaster had the perfect formula for success. His plan was to regain control of the area into coalition's favor in record time and return control back to the Turkmen people. McMaster's Third Cavalry Regiment focused first on befriending the smaller surrounding cities while focusing on security to and from the nearby Syrian border located to the west. Securing the area between Tal Afar and the Syrian border would prevent weapons, supplies, and access routes for the enemy. In addition, McMaster built up a tough local fighting force and personally developed a strong trust with locals.

McMaster's focus of his forces and mission intent brought exactly what senior leadership, to include the White House, wanted in Iraq for the surge—befriend the local population, train the police and army, and develop a plan to eventually handover the area back to the government once the insurgency has been defeated.

The McMaster plan began with a little help from a Hoosier Army National Guard unit that had been recently deployed to Iraq, the 113th Engineer Company originally based out of Northern Indiana. The engineers were deployed to Iraq to support what was termed "Operation Restoring Rights." The Hoosiers were tasked by McMaster to build a massive man-made berm that enclosed Tal Afar that had fallen entirely under the control of the insurgency.

With protection from the 113 Engineer's critical berm, just over five thousand soldiers from the Iraqi Army's Third Division fought hard to take back Tal Afar from the enemy. The beaten enemy was pounded by Iraqi forces, cavalry air support, and a hard-hitting ground attack from all directions thanks to the protective berm that was erected under tough enemy fire. Later, Tal Afar mayor Najim Abdullah al-Jubouri sent praises to President Bush for McMaster's Third Cavalry Regiment and the 113th Engineers. The soldiers of the Indiana Army National Guard's 113th Engineer Company lived up to their treasured motto of "service and fidelity" for McMaster that sealed victory in the fight for Tal Afar.

But the current situation in Iraq was no longer considered in control. McMaster's Tal Afar victory happened several years prior to our arrival in Iraq, and something quickly had to be done for coalition forces to regain the upper hand in Iraq as Operation Restoring Rights did. McMaster's successes during his career were highly praised, and his position on the council of colonels was specifically requested by the chiefs. Once alerted to join the council, McMaster bolted from his home base at Fort Riley, Kansas, and reported to The Pentagon for his new tasking. A tasking he savored as a former ground commander in Iraq.

President Bush spoke of the current Iraqi situation in December of 2006. The president said, "I am listening to a lot of advice to develop a strategy to help (Iraq) succeed, a lot of consultations. I will be delivering my plans after a long deliberation, after steady deliberation. But I'm not going to be rushed into making a decision." But his mind was defiantly set on a rapid troop increase. Details were on the way.

Following the speech, former vice of the Joint Chiefs Jack Keane met with President Bush with a report on Gen. Peter Pace. Keane admitted to the president that Pace had been given a "failing grade" as the current chairman of the Joint Chiefs. This grade traumatically bothered and disturbed the four-star Marine Corps general, and Pace was devastated in disbelief of the harsh grade by the former vice. Meanwhile, Iraq's ground commander General Casey felt totally disrespected that he was being completely left out of any decision-making or planning. New plans were evolving from Washington, and a massive troop surge was being orchestrated without Casey's input, advice, or accord. Casey felt pushed to the side, his authority overridden, and he felt completely belittled in front of the world.

In addition to the president hearing of failing grades regarding his highest level of generals, public opinion was dwindling with the war in Iraq, and the political landscape was tilting against the Republican Party and White House as bad news continued to pour from the troubled country. The war effort was slowly sinking into chaos.

President Bush continued with the increase of troops planning. But there were problems and issues to deal with as deployment orders were being published. Units had been extended with little or no notice. Soldiers had completed multiple tough deployments and ordered to return to the combat zone. Existing equipment had been heavily used, abused, and beaten. Units were issued and being deployed with broken and depleted equipment that had been dragged across the planet several times, simply tattered from previous combat tours, leaving materials in poor condition. The Pentagon and Department of Defense were fully aware if these awful facts but were forced to march on with the president's strict orders.

National Guard units such as the Thirty-Fourth Infantry based out of Minnesota, but now at Al-Taqaddum (an air base known as TQ) located in the southern part of the Al Anbar Province were told to stay in place for an additional four grueling months. The Thirty-Fourth "Red Bull Division" had been away from home for nearly two exhausting years, training for and serving in Iraq. I did not look forward to pulling into TQ's main gate and greeting the Red Bull guys who were there well over a year with several months remaining until returning back to the states. The Thirty-Fourth mechanics were often tasked with repairing our battered Humvees and other vehicles in Iraq. And the Red Bull mechanics somehow managed to keep our gun trucks rolling and mission ready.

The Thirty-Fourth guys always kept up a great attitude and drove on strong, even with the forced extension. The Red Bull soldiers worked long hot days with an every-day-is-the-same style of mission, but the Thirty-Fourth stood proud and without complaint or sighs. They were great soldiers to serve with, and I always went out of my way to greet them and asked if anything was needed. Strange, the Red Bull guys never needed anything. They had great attitudes and always had a smile.

Following an evening company briefing, I was briefed on vehicle mission status. The 152nd trucks were being deadlined due to bullet-ridden windshields. I wanted to see firsthand what was the problem from our top mechanic who would always tell me how it was without bullshit, Marc Laddy. But we were out of replacement windshields, and new windshields were on back-order.

Humvee trucks in Iraq had windshields that were made of two inches of thick protective glass, a solid glass that could easily absorb a medium-sized machine gun bullet. And our trucks were being sniped, blasted, and pelted with bullets daily.

That evening, I walked down a dusty Camp Ramadi road from the 152nd company operations shack to talk to Laddy about the windshield situation. Our company was completely out of usable windshields, and trucks were still running missions through and around Ar Ramadi with shattered windshields that were nearly impossible to see out of. Sergeant First Class Laddy and I decided we needed to drag the least bullet-ridden windshields that had once been removed from our gun trucks and returned the less damaged windshields to gun trucks for the next day's missions.

Windshields with two or three bullet holes were easier to see out of than a windshield with twenty or thirty bullet holes.

"This is the best we can do." Laddy sighed while staring at a pile of shattered Hummer windshields. "New windshields are on order, and we cannot order them fast enough." It was clear Laddy wanted to do more and say "mission complete," but he could not. This bothered the senior noncommissioned officer whom I had worked so closely with over the past three years.

We both sorted the best windshields from the pile of slightly damaged windshields over the next few days and placed them back on gun trucks. This was a temporary fix for a tough combat mission.

The bullet-ridden windshields were a grim reminder for me of how just how dangerous and deadly the Ar Ramadi area was. It was very dangerous, but we strolled through hell's darkest chambers without hesitation or fear every day.

I made it a point to join convoy briefs each morning and just stand with 152nd soldiers as they prepped to move out to police stations, asking platoon leaders if they needed anything…except new windshields. Windshields were on order. If possible, I would join convoys to take the deadly voyage through Ar Ramadi, even if I had no task or reason to be with the traveling platoon. It was difficult to see where we were going through the shattered and bullet-ridden windshields, but I went.

We had several trucks with major IED damage and quickly repaired them within days to rejoin the fight. But the damage to our vehicles was not the only casualty in the 152nd. The battle was taking its toll on our cyclone soldiers. One soldier with first platoon was certain he was a "bad luck charm" for any convoy he patrolled with.

"We are going to get hit…" the bad charm soldier would mumble during a pre-convoy brief. "We are going to get hit," he continued to mumble over and over.

Most of the 152nd guys would just blow his words off and soon ramble down one of Ramadi's dusty and dangerous roads. But the haunting words slurred from the self-described bad luck charm was troubling, specifically after hearing the squad took hits that day. But all of our squads were taking hits every day. Every mission.

Several of our younger soldiers were also deeply affected by the daily and deadly missions in Ar Ramadi. Some would sit near the back doors of their wooden shacks in complete silence and stare into the distance. Each day was deadly and dangerous.

The mission was taking its physical and emotional toll on our Indiana Army National Guard unit. I did not want us to evolve into the Three-Hundredth and become the unwanted unit of Camp Ramadi or let down the Ready First team that warmly welcomed us to the remote base in Iraq's "wild west."

The "wild west" is what Captain Henton first described Ar Ramadi to me as we arrived in Iraq, and he was right. Ar Ramadi was, in fact, the "wild west."

GENERAL PEACHES

As Casey took control of the Iraq War effort in 2005, the general was desperate that the Iraqi elections would lead to a unified and less violent country under his watch, specifically with recent training of Iraqi security forces. And Casey thought his plan would create a sharp reduction of US troop withdrawals as early as spring 2006, but that did not happen for Casey. Casualty rates increased, the number of coalition forces did not dwindle, and the American people were frustrated with what seemed to be a never-ending war at a high cost in dollars, as well as a high cost in American lives. Even the Iraqi people were becoming disgruntled with coalition forces as the insurgency grew stronger and bolder.

Casey was simply frustrated and distraught with the complete loss of control in Iraq. He knew Washington was drawing plans to change the war's direction in Iraq, and Casey became reclusive and paranoid.

Iraqi security forces were easily bribable, poorly trained and equipped. But of all things, they were tribal and stuck together. For coalition forces to step away would be traumatic for Iraq and the Iraqi people. Rice described the Iraqi Police as "abusive" at times and would not lay complete trust in them. She knew the Iraqi Army would work for anyone who paid and fed them, but they were fighting for us at the time, so all was good on that side of the house.

As talks of increasing troop numbers in Iraq continued, Casey remained against the thought and would cringe at the fact that numbers were not decreasing. Casey continued to press his plan of a victory by timetable to the White House with hope that things would just work out somehow. The Casey "Take 3" approach to victory was being frowned upon by President Bush, as well as members of the Joint Chiefs of Staff, specifically Chairman General Pace.

Pace was known to ironically pace the floor of his Pentagon's office regarding the fact that Iraq was failing. He knew changes were needed and needed fast.

President Bush was briefed several times each day at this point of the war, but each brief concluded with the fact that the war was not tilting in the United States' favor. The insurgency owned the roads and terrorized Baghdad, Anbar, small towns, and the farming communities throughout Iraq. Casey's removal as Iraq's senior commander was now in President Bush's near radar, and the president was eager at this point to remove Casey swiftly but without humiliating the four-star general that America continued to have a favorable opinion of. But the president knew it was time for a change at the top in Baghdad.

Casey, always with his sharp, perfectly ironed uniform and wire-rimmed glasses, graduated from Georgetown University in 1970, and was commission with Georgetown's ROTC program. But Casey did not follow in his father's military footsteps to become a commissioned officer. Casey joined the ROTC program, and his father graduated from West Point, later serving as a general-grade army officer in Vietnam. The younger Casey preferred to live in the Washington DC area and was accepted at the private university, Georgetown. The senior Casey, who fought in World War II and Korea was later killed in Vietnam while commanding the army's beloved First Cavalry Division, preferred the combat zone. While traveling by helicopter in South Vietnam to visit wounded soldiers, the senior Casey died while the helicopter he was piloting hit a mountainside due to poor weather and visibility near Bao Luc. This tragedy occurred just prior to the junior Casey's commission at Georgetown University. The newly commissioned Casey was devastated by his father's death but continued to serve and climb up the ranks in the army quickly with a spotless record. Casey completed the army's prestigious Ranger School following his promotion to second lieutenant and earned the wings of a master parachutist. Everything went right for Casey during his impressive career, except as commanding general of Operation Iraqi Freedom.

Casey eventually conceded to the president's order to increase the number of soldiers in Iraq. Reluctantly, the four-star general delivered a four-point plan to his staff that included a bulky additional increase in troop strength, but he again included another timeline. This timeline was something President Bush did not know about or authorize to Casey to deliver to his staff. Casey's timeline allowed a ninety-day limit to pass control of Iraq to the government.

The president was furious.

Another Iraqi timeline was not what President Bush wanted. He wanted solid results without time limits, and the commander in chief wanted results immediately.

President Bush turned to Gen. John Abizaid who was in charge of Central Command that oversaw responsibilities in twenty-six Middle East countries that included Iraq. President Bush shared his frustration with Abizaid regarding Casey's timelines and failures, but Abizaid was on Casey's side. Abizaid was also against the increase of soldiers in Iraq, and this enraged the commander in chief.

A West Point graduate, Abizaid's career dates back to Operation Urgent Fury, the 1983 deployment to Grenada ordered by then president Ronald Reagan. Abizaid was a company commander with the US Army Rangers during the American invasion of Grenada. After parachuting onto a remote airstrip in Grenada, Abizaid ordered a few of his rangers to drive a bulldozer toward enemy Cuban troops as he and his soldiers advanced behind the dozer's protection, a move highlighted in the 1986 movie, *Heartbreak Ridge*, starred and directed by Hollywood icon Clint Eastwood.

The president was not amused by General Abizaid's support of Casey. The president wanted General Abizaid to concur with his plan to increase numbers in Iraq and swiftly change strategy. Sadly, General Abizaid retired three months following his briefing regarding Casey and troop increases with President Bush. General Abizaid's military career and personal life quietly faded away.

Casey's dream of witnessing troop levels drop from 140,000 to 100,000 by spring of 2006 did not evolve, and the upcoming troop swell was evolving without the general's input or knowledge. President Bush relieved the discouraged commanding general of his post, and Casey quietly departed Iraq on a small twin-engine plane reserved for high-ranking generals and returned to the states not knowing what his military future would hold. Casey was silent and ashamed following his hasty departure from the Baghdad International Airport. There was no brilliant ceremony, no marching band, and no medals to pin on the chest of his impeccably ironed uniform. He just left in the middle of the night minus any fanfare or glitter in which he lived for.

Casey was warned by his deputy, Lt. Gen. Peter Chiarelli, of being removed following the disastrous midterm elections that cost the Republican Party loss of power in congress. On a cold January morning of 2007, the United States House of Representatives' wooden gavel was passed on from the reluctant leader of the house, Dennis Hastert, to ultraliberal Californian representative Nancy Pelosi. President Bush felt blindsided and punished following his loss of power in congress. Changes were needed and needed quickly.

Following the change in congressional leadership, the president ordered Gen. David Petraeus to now lead Iraq. The newly promoted four-star general was selected to take charge of the new mission in Iraq, and he was to bring in the surge.

Petraeus was a very proud West Point graduate, who graduated top of his class in 1974 and moved up the promotion chain with a very successful and rapid rate. Although nicknamed "Peaches" by his peers for his boyish looks, General Petraeus's career was destined for success. He earned the General George C. Marshall Award at West Point and later received top graduate honors of the US Army Command and General Staff College in 1983.

Petraeus understood that security of the population and building a close partnership with the Iraqi Police would be the primary effort for his plan to return the Iraqi fight to coalition control. A tough plan required a constant military presence primarily in Baghdad's most dangerous neighborhoods. The new commanding general placed an intensive focus on helping Iraq improve its governmental efficiency, develop new employment programs, and improve overall life for citizen of Iraq.

General Petraeus was well aware that Iraqi tribal leaders were growing frustrated with Al-Qaeda. He had plenty of experience in Iraq prior to taking command and took full advantage of the enemy's current weakness to exploit it in any and every way possible. A "tilt back" to victory was in the general's crosshairs.

President Bush promoted Petraeus to lieutenant general in 2004, and the new three-star was selected as the first commander of the Multinational Security Transition Command of Iraq. This novel Iraqi command position for Petraeus made him responsible for training, equipping, and mentoring the country's army and police forces. Petraeus's second task was directed to improving training facilities, adding police stations throughout Iraq, and tightening border security specifically with Syria to the west of Iraq.

General Petraeus was the complete opposite of Casey, never craving attention or praise. The general only wanted success, and he didn't mind a fine layer of dust on his camouflage or a slab of mud under his boots. Petraeus was also very driven and eager to return the Iraqi fight back to coalition control and deliver victory for President Bush. The president was instantly impressed by Petraeus, and progress seemed immediate.

Peaches was perfect for the job at hand.

Following General Casey being relieved of duty in Iraq and placing Petraeus to lead the way in Iraq, President Bush graciously tapped Casey for the position of chief of staff of the army. The senate easily confirmed Casey's nomination as chief on February 8, 2007, but the disappointed general did not relish the fact of being removed from a senior command position to a powerless staff job in Washington.

Duty for Casey in Washington meant not commanding thousands of soldiers with a huge command staff nor a prestigious position in the Pentagon. Casey was now a staffer in political Washington, DC. Most generals moving from a four-star command such as Iraq's senior leader went on to head Central Command or other glamorous command positions or an honorable spot within the Joint Chiefs' office. Instead, he was to deal with army training, administrative duties, and plenty of briefings to yawn through with endless cheesy photo ops and horse and pony shows to attend. Casey despised this position but accepted it although he felt demoted and ashamed.

Another victim of Casey's removal was Lieutenant General Chiarelli's. His career never recovered from the Iraqi disaster.

The House of Representatives managed to pass a colossal $125 billion spending bill by a narrow ten-vote difference in April to keep the war machine rolling, and the funding of "the Iraqi surge" was approved under the leadership of House Leader Pelosi. The US Senate also ratified funding for the Iraq War. The war continued to roll.

TRIANGLE OF DEATH

nsurgents hated us more than anyone or anything…at least that is what we were told. We were told *they* were the "insurgents." Maybe *we* were the insurgents, I don't know…but that is what we called them and what we were told they were…insurgents. But overall, they hated us and hated us for being here. And the insurgency hated the simple fact that Americans were working, fighting, and living side by side with the Iraqi police and Iraqi army. We trained the Iraqi Police; we armed the IPs, ate with the IPs, and lived with the IPs. We even fought with the IPs. They eventually became loyal to us as we did them, completely trusted, met every day as coworkers, and above all, we were friends, friends in what was considered the heart of the Iraqi "Triangle of Death."

The Triangle of Death's name evolved from recent and fierce insurgency attacks directed against coalition in a certain area, a triangle pattern. The triangle consisted of terrain that favored guerrilla-style fighting, hasty attacks, and roadside bombs. The Triangle's far north point was near the town of Baiji, far left of the deadly Triangle was our new location of Ar Ramadi, and the far-right point of the triangle went just east of Baghdad. The area within this deadly Triangle lived approximately one million Iraqis, primarily Sunnis, comprised of several large towns in the Mahmudiya District that included Yusufiyah, Mahmoudiyah, Iskandariyah, Latifiya, and Jurf Al Sakhar. The region is encompassed with hundreds of small rural villages and farming areas, family-worked farms that were fed by the many canals spawning off the mighty Euphrates River that ran along the southern border of the feared Iraqi Triangle of Death.

Our company was spread out along the key terrain feature of the Triangle of Death, the historic Euphrates River. This area is where bloody enemy attacks had sharply increased over that past twelve months, specifically on Route Mobile west of Fallujah. After insurgents would launch their swift attacks, then they could escape into the many small villages, hiding and blending in with the populace with ease. Rugged dirt roads and tricky canals were often riddled with buried bombs or IEDs that insurgents could easily conceal. Insurgents could also easily escape into the many canal systems following an attack or easily place roadside bombs on Route Mobile at night under the disguise of darkness. While on convoy between Baghdad and Ramadi, recent blast marks and craters could be seen easily. The scorched and damaged pavement seemed as if we were looking at ghosts, not knowing exactly what happened or what lives were lost at the unnerving stretch of road. I would rub my eyes and try to refocus at the roadside destruction to clear my mind. But that would not remedy the horrible thoughts of the blasted roadside and twisted guardrails. Destruction and death sat as reminders along Route Michigan as we convoyed, hoping we would not be the next victims of a deadly roadside bomb or IED.

Roadside IEDs reminded us of how much the insurgents despised us. And most of the American grunts on ground didn't really blame them. We were on their Iraqi turf, hiring, leading, and training Iraqis to defend themselves and fight to take back their own neighborhoods that they and their families lived in. Spotting and clearing IEDs were something every level of command demanded we were trained on and were focused on. Roadside bombs were killing and wounding with great accuracy. Jamming devices were added to gun trucks to block blasting devices. Videos were distributed to help convoy leaders spot possible threats. Convoys with blinding spotlights slowly crept along roads at night to clear highways of IEDs that coalition forces used, but IEDs continued to blast at convoys and kill coalition on a daily basis. The insurgency thrived on intimidating both coalition and the public.

To weaken the IED threat, Lt. Gen. Stanley McChrystal arrived in Iraq as the superior officer of the Multinational Security Transition Command. And bringing in the surge was Petraeus's main effort, and victory meant we had to minimize the IED threat. McChrystal worked well with the new theater commander and focused primarily on fixing the Baghdad area, as well as the Al Anbar Province with the addition of troops in Iraq. Squashing the IED threat was crucial for McChrystal, as well as his friend and Iraq's new commanding general "Peaches" Petraeus.

Like Petraeus, McChrystal was also a West Point graduate, class of 1976, and he had plenty of combat experience. While serving in Afghanistan, McChrystal was criticized following the 2004 death of Army Ranger and former professional football star Pat Tillman of the National Football League's Arizona Cardinals. Within a day of Tillman's death, McChrystal was aware that the former NFL star fell victim to friendly fire, but McChrystal attempted to bury the bad news. He knew that he was in line for a significant promotion in Iraq to assist with the surge. So the up-and-coming general tried to bury the dreadful news unsuccessfully. He survived the trauma with a few bumps, but he somehow managed to move on with his military career, earning a third star.

McChrystal was a very effective commander of the prestigious Joint Special Operations Command that boosted his choice for the key three-star position in Iraq. While commander of Special Operations, he was credited with the death of Abu Musab al-Zarqawi, the then leader of Al-Qaeda operating in Iraq. McChrystal earned high praises from senior leadership in Washington for his accomplishments with the Special Operations command. He was the shining star in Iraq and making progress in huge ways.

Following with the devastating death of the kingpin Abu Musab al-Zarqawi, McChrystal then began to focus on the lowest level in Iraq, the police stations and the Americans working and living with the police. The Iraqi Army and Iraqi Police were needed to take on the insurgency. In many ways, Iraq mirrored the American Civil War, fought only 150 years ago on American soil. North versus South, state versus state, brother versus brother. And some of the Iraqi hatred ran deep and strong. Again, very much like the brutal and bloody American Civil War that lingered in America for years and years.

To make this happen, the Americans had to begin working closer with the IPs, living with the IPs, deeply embedded as we were told and instructed to do. And we were there for the long haul, it seemed. Embedded Americans was something the new Iraqi commander stressed and wanted badly.

But working with the IPs or Iraqi Army was dangerous. It was a well-known fact that platoon leaders had a decent bounty on their heads. This price was equal to $1,500 American dollars. But this amount of $1,500 was a one-year wage for most Iraqis. The bounty seemed shallow, but to an Iraqi, that was enough cash to house and feed a family for many, many months. Money seemed to rule the country, whether dirty money or well-earned. Cash was simply king.

But day-to-day duty with the Iraqi Police was not easy. Coalition forces assigned to Iraqi security forces usually related working with the Iraqi Police as to herding cats or pushing wet cement. And this was an honest, truthful, solid Iraqi fact. However, the IPs were deep down great fighters. They grew up fighting with all types of weapons, war, and bloodshed. This was simply a way of life for them. A machine gun in their hands and a few thousand rounds of ammunition, the party was on. During a fight, we trainers would sit back, usually in a fire support position and just watch the fireworks show.

An Iraqi firefight was an amazing sight for the Americans assigned with their IP counterparts. What an American Army platoon would use in ammunition, flares, grenades, multiply that by fifty or sixty or maybe more. Americans called that "Iraqi math." Send a resupply mission as the fight begins, and we may be able to rearm an Iraqi Police unit as they run out of ammunition during the initial blast. This was mainly to blame as a part of Iraqi fighting customs. Just send lead down range and send it and send it and send it. At times, support troops behind the IPs could hear and see tracer rounds from the IPs coming in the opposite direction of their fight. It was simply amazing, yet terrifying. When patrolling with a group of police, watch your front, left, right, and rear. It is just that way. There's little we could do to change or alter this, regardless of how hard you try, threaten, or demand. It was just that way, and our higher command desperately wanted this fact changed and fixed, but how can you fix a culture and mindset during the matter of months or weeks?

An Iraqi "Death Star" was a perfect example of an outrageous fighting technique. Five or six Iraqis in a circle, facing outward, shoulder to shoulder, and firing as fast as possible.

We also had concerns of the IPs and who they *really* were. We wanted to trust them, but we were always cautious. The Three-Hundredth told us the story of an IP gate guard who allowed a suicide bomber into the police station just to the south of Camp Ramadi. The gate guard was paid several hundred American dollars for the evil task. The IP manning the gate who allowed the car in the station was seen walking south into the desert, following the deadly blast, and was never seen again. Rumor was he went to Baghdad and slipped away from existence.

The Iraqis could fight in a bath towel and slippers if needed. IPs could fire any weapon imaginable and send thousands of rounds in any direction. They could fight and fight and fight. They also enjoyed using bullhorns. Even calling their enemy out to fight while they were in hiding or full retreat was the norm. We knew when they insulted insurgents, the Iraqi junior enlisted, or shirtas, would laugh and laugh.

Our interpreters would explain, "The chief just called them chicken asses!"

We were assigned to the Al Anbar Province, covering Fallujah, Ramadi, and Habbaniya. These areas were deep Sunni country, and Former Iraqi Dictator Saddam Hussain was Sunni, and locals continued to worship and praise the former Iraqi president who was now in coalition custody. We had to be careful of what we said and did around the Iraqis in this area of the region. Some Iraqis still carried photos of their hero Saddam in their pockets. Some bragged about all the great things Saddam did for the Anbar Province and Sunni people. Sunnis bragged about apartment buildings Saddam ordered built or water supply lines laid, military complexes erected, and whatever else that was built during the former president's rule over Iraq.

Following his inauguration, Saddam ordered all types of construction throughout the Ramadi and Fallujah areas. For Iraq, they were once very nice, well-built structures. Some apartment complexes were built seven-stories high with beautiful courtyards and elaborate gardens. However, most of the impressive and well-constructed buildings were now ridden with bullet holes, sloppy patchwork-covered rocket-propelled grenade craters, and most roads had been heavily damaged by several years of war. Most of the septic and waterlines in Anbar had been destroyed or broken beyond repair. The region was in despair and totally destroyed.

We were in the epicenter of the Al Anbar Province, Ar Ramadi, during the close of the Saddam trials. We did not show emotion regarding Saddam's capture, court hearings, or eventual death by hanging. Most of the local Iraqi employees on Camp Ramadi lived close by. They ran what we called the "hajji shops" on the camp. They sold illegally copied American movies for a few bucks each. Some movies were just released in theaters, but they somehow had them on sale in fancy wrapping with colorful discs. Don't know how they got them, but they had dozens of brand-new movie releases that had not even been seen in American theaters. These shops also had Cuban cigars. Well, Cuban-made according to Iraqi storeowners.

Americans think the word *hajji* is a horrible or insulting word to call the Iraqis. But it is considered a compliment to an older Iraqi who has completed the voyage or hajji to Mecca. Therefore, if you have completed the hajji, you are a hajji. However, the Western view regarding the term *hajji* is usually used as an insult. It depends on how it is addressed. It can be a compliment or an insult. Americans were instructed to avoid the term, but it was how we identified things, the hajji shop, the hajji police, and so on.

After our arrival at Camp Ramadi, it seemed that we had a very good, positive relationship with the local people of Ar Ramadi and the IPs. This was something top brass in theater and generals back in The Pentagon strongly wanted in order for the surge's success although IEDs and enemy snipers were creating havoc throughout the region in staggering numbers.

Our best ally in Ramadi was a young sheikh and hero to the people of the Al Anbar Province named Sheikh Abdul Sattar Eftikhan al-Rishawi. To us, he was known as Sheikh Sattar, a thirty-five-year-old Sunni but was more of a prince or a man of local royalty. Sattar was highly respected for his business mind who employed many locals in the Ramadi area. Sattar ran the Sunni-dominant province with a highly valued authoritative style of leadership. He led the Anbar Province as a governor or mayor would of a large American city, and Colonel MacFarland desperately needed Sattar's friendship and trust of the local hero.

Sattar was also known for his fantastic diplomatic skills, combined with a deep desire to work with coalition forces to rid his area of terrorism. Sattar despised Al-Qaeda and its fear that grew like an evil plague in his treasured province. His home was located just inside the northern perimeter of Camp Ramadi, and he lived with his family that included five young children. Sattar was very proud of his family and always included his children in everyday events. The young Sheikh owned camels, sheep, and rams, and his palace was surrounded with beautiful gardens, huge palm trees that bordered his beautiful home's perimeter that included date trees and a lush watermelon patch. The back of his property included a nice view of the Euphrates River that snaked between Camp Ramadi and Camp Blue Diamond. Sheikh Sattar's best quality was that he had a close and personal relationship with all of the American battalion and brigade commanders in the region and his gentle ways and grace dazzled coalition leadership, as well as the Ramadi people during this difficult time.

The 152nd commander, Capt. Dan Henton, and I were at the mindset that we had to be trusted and welcomed by the local police and IP leadership. Leadership at the main Ramadi police station did not like their former mentors, the Three-Hundredth, that were assigned to Ar Ramadi prior to our arrival. The Three-Hundredth had several female MPs that thought little of the Iraqi Police. Key Three-Hundredth leadership were hard to find and not loyal to the IP struggles regarding retention, pay, equipment, and supplies crucial to everyday business. Henton always kept a close personal relationship with IP leaders and his mission to make the station, as well as the surge, successful. Henton was a hands-on guy with a mission-first attitude. He strived to never quit, and that failure was simply not an option. Henton and Sattar quickly became friends, and they were always together at the station during visits or trouble.

Sattar had a long deep history in the Arabic world. The sheikh was the grandson of a key tribal military leader during the Iraqi revolt against British occupying forces in 1920. Sattar was also the son of an Iraqi military commander from the Anglo-Iraqi War of 1941. And Sattar was not to give into Al-Qaeda thugs who were kidnapping and beheading tribal Sunnis as part of a campaign of extortion and intimidation that had tightened their evil grip on the Anbar Province. Al-Qaeda also had its sights on the local population as well. Kidnapping brought a high ransom that was usually paid quickly. Typically, men were abducted with ages ranging from seventeen to twenty-one. Family members knew that their loved ones would not return if ransom money were not delivered quickly.

As a local leader, life was very dangerous for Sheikh Sattar and other Iraqis who supported the coalition. Sattar's father and three brothers had already been killed by Al-Qaeda prior to our unit's arrival. This built the sheik's desire to destroy and end Al-Qaeda in Iraq and his province. But sadly, Sattar's partnership with the Americans would bring an end to his young successful life. A car bomb killed Sattar in late December near his home. The blast killed his driver and bodyguard, as well as injured two of Sattar's children who were playing nearby. The fatal blast was felt for miles, and the killing inflamed the IPs and locals who adored Sattar.

I concurred with Henton's intent to work as close to the IPs as possible despite the tragic loss of Sattar and earn their trust. Gain the trust of the IPs, gain the trust of the locals, and that would create a winning edge. With the initial invasion of Iraq considered old news, a new Iraqi policy was drawn up from the highest levels to work with Iraqi Police and Iraqi Army took an up close and personal outreach. And that was what we were going to do. We had to and wanted to.

The book, *Dereliction of Duty: Lyndon Johnson, Robert McNamara, The Joint Chiefs of Staff, and the Lies that Led to Vietnam*, was a great tool for us as embedded liaisons to learn from. McMaster's book, now a suggested read by the army, was based on his PhD dissertation at the University of North Carolina, and the book was nothing less than brutal and to the harsh point of reality. Along with the book's theme that the military is to be used appropriately in order to meet objective military targets and goals—something that was sure to make McMaster cringe as Casey's plans had timetables with hopes of elections winning wars—and focus on winning. In the 1997 book, McMaster carefully detailed why military actions in Vietnam failed to *resolve* or *communicate*. Missions ultimately fail when trying to accomplish sparsely detailed, confusing, and conflicting military objectives such as Vietnam or Iraq in 2006 under Casey's watch. McMaster stressed it was the military's responsibility during Vietnam to confront high-level civilian bosses when current strategy was not working. It seemed as we were beginning to slip back into a Vietnam type of war in Iraq in 2006, a war with only hopes and timelines to fight by. Much like the Vietnam War that McMaster remembered watching on the six o'clock news each evening as a kid on his family's living room RCA television set.

Overall, the best learning tool from the book is working with the locals and earning their trust. That is what we needed to do and had to do. McMaster was a role model for me, and I took his approach to the locals personally.

McMaster's motivator for writing his book, *Dereliction of Duty*, evolved from his studying accounts of the Vietnam War while at West Point as a young cadet. Many of the staff at West Point who taught McMaster were Vietnam veterans, most from the officer side of the army.

The war in Vietnam "was not lost in the field, nor was it lost on the front pages of *The New York Times* or on the college campuses. It was lost in Washington, DC," he wrote. McMaster blamed total human failure, the responsibility for which was shared by President Johnson and both his principal military generals and civilian advisors. Overall, the Vietnam War was lost in DC.

Following McMaster's return from Iraq in February of 2006, the chairman of the Joint Chiefs General Pace and his fellow Joint Chiefs requested debriefings from senior field commanders, specifically Colonel McMaster who had recently led in Iraq or Afghanistan. Pace was fascinated with McMaster's success in Tel Afar and desperately wanted his staff to listen and learn from the decorated colonel.

McMaster would eventually rise to the rank of lieutenant general and also serve in Afghanistan. He would later be appointed to the position of National Security Advisor within the president Donald Trump administration in 2017.

Overall, the success McMaster accumulated in Tal Afar is what we wanted in Ramadi.

OPERATION BUTTERCUP

Our infantry company was quickly settling in with Ready First and our seven police stations in the troubled province. Police recruiting numbers began to jump with our aggressive style of bringing in new candidates. We were enthusiastic and eager to recruit and train the IPs and increase each station's numbers and bring in new and improved material and equipment. Some stations were in decent shape with around-the-clock electricity and running water, but a few were in horrible shape. We were out to improve each station and aggressively continue with quality IP recruiting. It did not take long until the First Brigade's leadership became impressed with our willingness to work with the IPs. Soon, the 152nd was told additional stations and checkpoints would be added to our workload. One key location was in Tameem, not far from Camp Ramadi's south gate.

Shortly after we arrived at Camp Ramadi, I was told that our company was to be included in a sweep-and-clear operation through the Tameem area of Al Ramadi. The small community of Tameem is located on the southwest corner of Al Ramadi and was considered a decent area to live in although the poverty and unemployment rate were incredibly high. Exactly how the people of Ar Ramadi actually survived was unknown to me. Each family was entitled to a certain amount of food per day, pita bread, flour, sugar, and a few other items to live by. But with these items, life was overall rough for a majority of Ar Ramadi families.

The upcoming Tameem sweep was to be called "Operation Buttercup" and would involve a majority of our Infantry unit, one hundred IPs from several police stations, three navy SEAL snipers, a few dozen marines, and the air force that would provide air cover during the ground sweep. A company-size unit from the Anbar Iraqi Army was also used, but they kept a very low profile. They were tasked to provide more of a support role for the operation. We were not sure why, but the Iraqi Army just tagged along to the rear of our sweep that was to start on the north side of Tameem and end on the south end of town on Route Michigan.

The roads getting to and around the Tameem area were some of the most dangerous and least liked to move about. This part of Ramadi was heavily populated and congested with narrow roads. Insurgents considered this a prime area to hit coalition vehicles with sniper shots or carefully placed IEDs that would always produce deadly results for the enemy.

Key coalition leaders traveled these dangerous roads often, and the insurgents knew it. Our leaders liked to have "eyes on" the city of Ramadi and the police stations, and leader's vehicles could be easily spotted. Six or several vehicles in a single movement was a dead give-away. Newer, freshly painted vehicles with clean windows were easy to spot from long distances. Insurgents were not stupid, just crafty and held several advantages such as they owned home turf, could hide in any crowd and blend in, and play dumb at a moment's notice…and play dumb very, very well.

Once we arrived at Camp Ramadi, a First Armored Division staffer came up to me and said, "Be careful going through the Tameem area. Tameem has plenty of great hiding spots for the insurgency. Just be very careful."

There was nothing special that coalition forces were looking for during Buttercup. This was a basic sweep of the fragile southwestern corner of Ar Ramadi. Fourth Platoon from our company had one specific mission during the sweep, and that was recon for a future police station to strengthen our presence in this vital area. I spearheaded the mission with Lt. Terry Bennick.

Lieutenant Bennick, who I referred to as TB, and I were much alike. We were former enlisted and later went off to officer candidate school, choosing infantry upon commissioning for our specialty branch. TB wanted to join the aviation branch following OCS, but the army needed infantry lieutenants, more grunts on the ground than helicopter aviators. TB had a beautiful bride at home and was a very religious man whom everyone admired. He was soft-spoken but always to the point. TB would always let his noncommissioned officers lead the platoon's soldiers while he planned and prepared for future missions.

The night prior to the sweep of the small city of Tameem, an operation order was to be delivered to the mission's leadership. We were to meet in a semiclassified room on Camp Ramadi that was named "The Hub." The operation order was ten-pages thick, and a large map was laid out on the floor of The Hub. The Hub resembled a fancy banquet room that the Iraqi Army once held ceremonies at and where luxurious meals were served. The map provided superb details of Tameem better than any diagram or computer-generated three-dimensional layout. Each building on the map had a block of wood or cardboard box over it. If a building was a school, it was clearly labeled and positioned on the floor as it actually was in its neighborhood. A religious masque was in the center of Tameem that we were planning to sweep. That too was clearly marked and had red tape placed on the floor, surrounding the building and ensuring all clearly took note of it. Americans entering a masque was a big mistake, and we clearly knew this fact. There were too many rules and guidelines regarding masques, so it was just best to not enter one or even get close to one. Let the IPs handle that task.

Earlier in the month, IPs chased down five insurgents who had hid in a masque in the Al Hurriya area located on the south side of Ramadi. I was with First Platoon that had joined in on the chase. As the IP trucks circled the masque, a squad of Iraqi Police swiftly stormed in the religious temple, dragging all five insurgents out. As the detained insurgents were being handcuffed and loaded into IP trucks, an Iraqi woman furiously tried to chase everyone off and away from the masque. The woman, waiving a homemade broom with both arms, was toting three small children behind her who were clinging onto her black outfit. The irate woman quickly grabbed our platoon's attention, but it was a very humorous moment for us as we attempted to keep a professional and hard stance as the IPs were loading up the five suspected insurgents.

We were taught a few words of Arabic during our buildup phase back in the states. Only two or three words were fully retained during our training back at Fort Dix. The American security team's sergeant began yelling, "IRSH-AH," meaning "get back." But the sergeant kept laughing as he was yelling the command to the hysteric Iraqi woman. The sergeant's corporal took over the verbal commands, attempting to get the old woman back in her house. The corporal took over mainly due to the sergeant was laughing so hard.

I was not sure exactly what the old woman was upset about. She could have been upset with Americans being so close to the masque, or that Iraqi Police were entering the masque to make the arrests. The arrested men could have been known or related to the broom-waiving Iraqi woman. I tried my best to be professional but admit that I began to laugh as well. However, I did a better job holding in my laughter than the sergeant. The IPs and Americans bolted out of the neighborhood in a quick and rapid manor, leaving the old woman screaming at us as we left, still waving her broom in the air.

The size of the map at The Hub was very impressive during the Buttercup operation order. Leaders gazed at city streets and alleyways as the briefing developed. The map allowed us to have a perfect bird's-eye view of the neighborhood streets and checked out what it will be like during the actual operation. As key leaders explained exactly where to be and how to go, they walked down the table's streets with long wooden pointers as details were explained. The city streets were marked with white tape, phase lines were colored bright yellow, and critical time lines were explained in great detail. It was a fantastic tool for the operation's planners. SEALs were to be deployed as snipers; their positions were marked with upside down white Dixie cups. The Dixie cups were marked with a large red X printed on the sides of each cup. The SEALs were to secretly crawl into place the night prior to the Tameem sweep and provide cover during Buttercup. Blue boxes represented where First Brigade's Bradley Fighting Vehicles were to be during the sweep. A large red rubber ball identified the command post, and next to the command post was a large red wooden block with no name or symbol. That was the casualty reference point but only lightly talked about during the briefing, not labeled. Labeling such a point meant bad luck, and we did not go into many details of a casualty collection point or CCP. Failure was not an option, and suffering losses was completely unacceptable. This reference was kept quiet and pushed to the side.

On the banquet room walls hung aerial photographs of Tameem, huge photos that were plastered from floor to ceiling. One photo detailed a certain building that stood alone…the soon-to-be Tameem Iraqi Police Station. Establishing a new station was the main purpose of this one-day mission called Buttercup. Leaders studied the photos while walking up and down the map's streets. They matched photos hung on walls to the floor's map, studying one to the other, then hovered over to the map on the floor to walk their course. Leaders stood to the side and discussed the best way to go through assigned areas and exactly who would go where according to the operation order. We dissected the area like a surgeon preparing a delicate heart surgery. The mammoth map on the floor gave commanders detailed information that a typical military map could not express. And the briefing in The Hub would later pay off for the next morning's mission known as "Buttercup."

We were to kick things off just as the sun came up on that rare chilly and frosty Iraqi morning. This was mid-January in Ramadi, so daybreak broke just after 6:00 a.m. as rows of soldiers, IPs, airmen, and SEALs prepped for Buttercup.

The 250-man detail that formed Operation Buttercup began with a few red cluster flares that arched over Tameem's apartment buildings that frigid January morning. Flares were the kickoff signal for us to move south through the municipal. Hummers and Bradley Fighting Vehicles revved up and dismounted soldiers, and Iraqi policemen marched south for the "Buttercup" sweep. The streets of Tameem were vacant and strangely quiet that morning. The two-mile-wide line of coalition soldiers and war machines didn't even see a mouse scamper that morning. It was deadly quiet, and it was bone-freezing as the sun was just beginning to rise over the city. Walking through the corridors of four-story apartments had everyone on their toes, even the Iraqis marching along with their AK-47 rifles were on the highest of attentiveness. Sometimes, silence resulted in a deadly day for coalition in built-up Iraqi city areas. As if the calm before the storm, everyone was cautious and on high alert.

On maps, Tameem streets look wider than they actually were. The streets in this section of Ramadi appeared to be alleys rather than streets that appeared or seemed to narrow, or perhaps the tunnel effect was playing games with me that morning. Apartment doors were shut tight, windows were closed and firmly curtained, but we knew plenty of eyes were on us from all around that morning.

With a few dozen IPs to our front and a squad of US Army riflemen flanking the right and left, all went according to schedule on that day. The giant map we studied the night prior was the perfect tool, providing a prime bird's-eye view. All the planning and coordinating in the banquet room saw its reward as the element continued to march south without flaw as the sun began to peak over a few buildings, adding just a little much-needed warmth to all in the sweep that morning.

What we knew as "Building H" was just a few hundred meters to our front. And in the quiet, I kept peering down a street named "Keeper" that led to the future police station that we were so desperate to locate.

Three of us from the 152nd approached the mysterious Building H, but I was unsure if we were in the correct location. I motioned for Sergeant Brawn to check out this odd-looking building to our front on Keeper.

"How is the roof standing?" I mumbled to Sergeant Brawn, who was as puzzled as I was with the sight of what he also guessed was Building H.

The building had been pummeled with bullets and littered with rocket damage. Rebar was strung everywhere from direct hits to the building, and the building's door was laying in the parking lot. I triple checked the map in my left hand.

"Yes, we are on Keeper," I stressed to Brawn. "I think…"

A few of the Iraqi Army soldiers who knew a few words of English strolled up as this was a walk in the park for them and explained that three large bombs had destroyed most of the building prior to our unit's arrival in Ramadi. Only one wall somehow remained upright, but the building somehow stood in the rubble remarkably. Insurgents had been told that this building was to become a police station, and they were to man what was left of this building as long as possible. To give up the building would be *nuts*. The building was empty but showed signs that someone had been living or working there as recent as that morning. A pile of blankets was thrown on the floor, and several teapots were left behind on a small table, still warm.

The silence was eerie as the last of the 152nd guys moved up and assembled around the future IP station. I was not sure what the purpose of this structure had served in recent years, but it was in horrible, horrible shape.

The operation ran smoothly without incident. In fact, the sweep went so well that the mission known as Buttercup was completed in record time, half the time originally planned to complete. I knew we were ahead of schedule as we crossed each phase line, but we were on the move with little or no delay or threat. During the operation order, about twenty to twenty-five Iraqis were in the banquet hall, and some lived nearby. The locals probably had relatives and friends in the area who were tipped off to stay out of the area or just lay low for a few hours. Word can spread as fast as a wildfire in Iraqi neighborhoods. With destroyed telephone lines and only the wealthy able to own automobiles, word could still spread quickly of coalition forces' plans and operations. We took this as a curse and as a blessing somehow.

Local Iraqi Police and Iraqi Army were allowed to participate in the brief the night prior to Buttercup at The Hub. They were to be involved, and on paper, they were to be considered apart of coalition forces and friendly. According to orders from higher-up, they had to be totally trusted in every way. This was their country, and some day they would take over control of the area without us. Take control once the war was won—if it ever was to be won. Even though it felt as though we were "sleeping with the enemy" at times, the Iraqi Police and Iraqi Army were to be included in everything…everything.

At Building H, I had thoughts of a *real* building to set up a police station. But this was a building of rubble, standing without doors, windows, or walls for protection. I pulled out a map from my cargo pocket to double-check its location. By this time, I was not worried about the enemy threat or watching my back. I, Sergeant Brawn, and a few riflemen just stared at the building in disbelief. I gave my map to Sergeant Brawn.

"You check it!" I asked. "Is this really the place? Or an abandoned building of rubble?"

"This can't be it?" added a rarely confused Brawn.

Staff Sergeant Brawn had been in both the active duty Army and National Guard for over twelve years. He was a smart noncommissioned officer with plenty of common sense that I laid plenty of trust in. I also relied on his guidance many, many times in the past. He excelled with the younger guys in the platoon and was always willing to provide advice both regarding the military and personal life for his subordinates. We had worked together for just over three years and had always saw things eye-to-eye. He was levelheaded and could always be relied on to give levelheaded advice with solid leadership in any condition or environment.

"This is it," Brawn announced as he continued to study the map in a voice as calm as could be. "This is the building, but I don't know why."

I walked in the building with Brawn, stepping over chunks of broken walls and rubble, avoiding dangling steel bars and electrical wiring hanging here and there from the ceiling that had a strange tilt from the recent bombarding. I knew the electricity was probably not working, but I was not to take any chances. We steered clear of the hanging wires and was cautious of every corner and room we cleared. Yes, eventually the building was labeled clear, and a green X was spray-painted on the southwest corner of the building to officially mark Building H was secure. But again, we were not taking any chances. I felt the southbound sweep had gone a bit too fast. Buildings were cleared in record time, too quickly for my thoughts. We remained cautious.

Regarding the sweep, either these guys were quick at clearing and were very good, or our element clearing Tameem's buildings and alleys were not checking each assigned area, not being very detailed about it. However, all units to me were dressed perfectly in-line and moving south as one solid unit.

After Sergeant Brawn and I left Building H, we felt in shock of its current horrible condition. How could this dump be the station that we would be operating out of and living in? It just did not seem right. Building H was just a pile of rubble.

Brawn called Building H a *dive* that he wouldn't let "his dog live in."

Our team left the wreckage of Building H to link up with a squad of IPs who were also involved in the Tameem sweep and quickly gathered on Route Michigan. Michigan was our furthest limit of advance to call the mission *green*. A pair of red flares streamed high over Route Michigan to confirm Operation Buttercup was complete, and the area was officially declared clear. As the red flares disappeared over the city, I looked back at Building H and noticed soldiers were already moving boxes and equipment into it. A large truck pulled up to Building H with twenty or thirty IPs stuffed in the cargo area. The IPs jumped from the truck's tailgate as diesel smoke rolled out of its exhaust just as the sun began to glare over several apartment buildings in Tameem, brightening the many ramshackle buildings in the city. The Iraqi policemen swarmed in the building once known as Building H, now officially the Tameem Police Station or TIPS. Within one hour of officially owning TIPS, two squads of

IPs strolled out of the station for their first official foot patrol through Tameem. One squad marched to the north side of town, the second to the south. The IPs went to work immediately and wanted to show the people that they meant business as official Tameem policemen.

I was very impressed with the eagerness of the IPs to begin patrolling Tameem. As both squads disappeared into the neighborhoods of the small corner of Ramadi termed Tameem, I was still unsure about the new station. I completely felt the station was unsuitable for anyone to live in. But the Iraqi policemen saw this building as a place of work, a way to support their families, bring stability to the city of Ramadi, and make TIPS a proud place to work out of.

Throughout the day, more and more trucks rolled into Tameem to supply the new police station with any possible bit of equipment and supply to ensure TIPS was as successful as possible. Additional policemen and crates of supplies to include Post-it notes constantly poured into the now vibrant station, and soon a small generator began to hum. The once abandoned building seemed to be magically brought back to life. As the day rolled on, a few spotlights glowed to illuminate the one-time pile of rubble that was only referred to as "Building H." For additional security, huge cement walls that were a whopping twelve inches thick were quickly set up and locked together. It seemed a new building was created around the tattered shanti miraculously in front of our very eyes. Amazingly it only took a few hours to show its true potential. Ready First meant business and made the station livable and safe to work out of in record time, pleasing the brigade commander and satisfying Lieutenant Colonel Lechner in every way. Both MacFarland and Lechner would keep close tabs on TIPS, knowing that controlling Tameem was vital in securing Ramadi and beyond. The enemy's running of cash, weapons, and equipment from Syria to Baghdad funneled through Ramadi, and Tameem was the focal point of its evil that overlooked Check Point Jones' vital intersection for the insurgency.

Iraqi and American troops would immediately live at the newly constructed Tameem Police Station, eat there, fight there, but mainly own a key position in the community of Tameem, a town that reflected the size of six or seven large city blocks. Premade gun towers rolled in on large American flatbed trucks, ready to set up and man quickly. IPs stacked sandbags to upgrade their fighting positions and gun towers. If they were not sturdy by nightfall, they could be shot, rocketed, sniped, whatever. Safety and security was key during these crucial first few days at TIPS. Things happen quick when your life is on the line, and the new Tameem Police Station was up and 100 percent operational within twelve short hours. It was amazing to see its construction set up so quickly and effectively. The station still looked a little ugly, and the fractured interior walls reminded all involved of what had happened and what could possibly happen to the small fortress that is now called *home.*

The station's small generator offered a bit of heat during the frigid Ramadi nights for the night staff, and security improved by the day. Overall, duty at TIPS was fairly quiet and uneventful. When an insurgent's hasty ambush hit, it was usually at night and from a far distance, producing no or little effect. IP teams would be dispatched to investigate any disturbance or potshot. The police were very protective of TIPS.

Lieutenant Starnes and his platoon were tasked to oversee the Tameem Iraqi Police Station. Third had a team showing up later in the day following TIPS's initial construction. Unsurprisingly, this task bothered Starnes. His station was the new hot spot, and this was prime territory that the insurgency didn't want coalition forces to own. The station was located northeast of the dreaded Check Point Jones, maybe a hundred yards or so away. And for the insurgency, Route Michigan was a major supply route that channeled weapons, cash, ammunition, trained snipers, and other goods into the Fallujah and Baghdad battlefield. This was crucial ground they wanted to keep.

Check Point Jones was a major intersection, constructed similar to a large decorative European roundabout. Check Point Jones was known to Iraqi locals as the Nazin Warrar Square. The checkpoint was indicatively the most dangerous spot in Ramadi to be near or to drive through, but we would not avoid the landmark Ar Ramadi roundabout. We were too proud to avoid it out of fear, and the roundabout was probably the most dangerous setting in the entire Anbar Province. Driving through Jones would make the hair on the back of my neck stand straight up, and driving through the checkpoint at night was intensively worse. Lieutenant Bennick had a rocket fly in front of his hummer's front windshield one night returning from his station, but TB's team could not fire back. Following current rules of engagement meant we needed two facts to return fire, a clear threat and a positive identification of the threat. TB didn't have the positive identification needed, and the team was forced to move through Check Point Jones without returning fire. Thoughtlessly firing into apartment complexes was unauthorized. Striking noncombatants or children sleeping in their beds was something we did not want to have happen; it was too risky.

The roundabout at Check Point Jones was a favorite for insurgent attacks. Coalition convoys were forced to slow down approaching the intersection although the size of the junction was large and easy to maneuver through. But this slowdown created an easy target for the enemy to take a shot at coalition vehicles driving by and then quickly disappearing into the city without being spotted.

Check Point Jones's position was vital ground to control in Ramadi, and Route Michigan was one of the several roads that split through the roundabout. A few miles north of Jones was the south entrance to Camp Ramadi. To the northeast continued Route Michigan that was a straight shot to Fallujah and then to Baghdad. To the north of the checkpoint was Route Jones. There was a sharp bend to Route Jones near the south gate of Camp Ramadi. The road shifted into an S pattern. It was very difficult to fight at this spot although coalition was so close to the safety of the camp. There were too many hiding places, plenty of alleys to duck into, with towering apartment buildings located on the east side of the road. The road ran wide at this bend on Route Jones for some reason but deadly. At this point on Jones, we were in the wide-open and simply easy targets. This was territory I dreaded driving through but did not refuse to convoy on. We had to show no fear although we did sink into our hummer's seats as we convoyed by, just hoping to survive.

RELUCTANT LIEUTENANT

Starnes was not thrilled about being assigned to the Tameem Police Station. There were always a few dozen Iraqi policemen at the station, and the lieutenant was okay with that. Starnes would rather stay at Camp Ramadi and just let the IP's run the station. I think the gym and the dining hall were more important to him than the IP mission that he was assigned to. While on a convoy with Staff Sergeant Brawn, just a few days after the Tameem sweep, we pulled into TIPS, an IP foot patrol was leaving the station to stroll through the dozen-or-so apartment complexes on the south end of the town. It was more of a presence patrol being conducted by the policemen or a basic security check. But I noticed that there were no American mentors or trainers with the patrol. I also took note that there were no Humvees in the parking area as well. There were no Americans advising, guiding, or directing…as ordered.

A few days later, Lieutenant Colonel Lechner called me to his office at his brigade headquarters on the north side of Camp Ramadi. The DCO was tasked by Colonel MacFarland to ensure the Iraqi police stations were successful, led, and mentored by their American liaison teams. But he felt one was not being assisted, as well as he was expecting. I was ordered to the DCO's office and to bring Lieutenant

Starnes with me. Lieutenant Colonel Lechner's office was also a wooden shack, much like our own company's dusty HQ shack. His so-called desk was made of plywood, and the desk was held together with a few rusty nails. Lieutenant Colonel Lechner did not need anything fancy to work or live out of. He was simply out to work hard and win. The Tameem Police Station had been open just over a week and running well, but the DCO liked to make personal visits to his many stations in the Ramadi area. Three visits in just as many days led to no sight or sound of the American IP team from the 152nd Infantry, specifically third platoon.

Lieutenant Colonel Lechner was seriously injured in Somalia with the Army Rangers during the 1993 Battle of Mogadishu or "Day of the Rangers." But the stalky, stern Lechner was always calm but direct to any point he wanted to make. The DCO firmly instructed Starnes to have Americans of his third platoon manning the station twenty-four hours a day.

"Be in place by midnight," Lechner calmly ordered Starnes from his dusty wooden desk.

Starnes stood silent. He took Lieutenant Colonel Lechner's instructions very, very hard. He did not want to be at the station that was assigned to his platoon or be in Tameem at all. Starnes was worried about paperwork and vehicle maintenance. Lieutenant Colonel Lechner instructed the lieutenant to complete the administrative tasks at the police station. "I will deliver a desk to your station for you," Lechner offered. "and there will be a maintenance team to assist your drivers if needed."

Starnes was speechless, his face was pale, and he was in pure shock as we left the "DCO" or deputy commanding officer shack.

The motto of the US Army Rangers is simple, "Rangers lead the way." And the lieutenant colonel wanted that with his IP teams in Ramadi, "Lead the way."

As Starnes and I were walking back to the 152nd headquarters area, Starnes said to me, "Well, it is four in the afternoon. I have eight hours to be there," I looked at Starnes and gladly offered to take over his platoon and run TIPS myself. I offered as calmly as the DCO spoke to the reluctant lieutenant just a few minutes earlier. Starnes did not like that proposal, and within a few hours, his platoon was lined up in the staging area next to our headquarters shack. Third platoon rolled out just after six o'clock with the unenthusiastic Starnes.

Starnes would have three different platoon sergeants during our time in Ramadi. His assigned platoon sergeants did not mix well with Starnes and his style of leadership.

Third platoon was tasked to assist the brigade's explosive ordinance detachment on a mission southwest of Ar Ramadi in early January, but Starnes was omitted from a brigade report and the lieutenant was visibly upset. His platoon was ordered to support the EOD team that was dissecting a flatbed truck loaded with explosives that was to eventually be used in an enemy suicide bomb attack. An anonymous tip was reported to the IPs of Ramadi's Main Police Station, and third platoon was ordered to provide overwatch while EOD defused the threat. However, lunchtime was nearing, and Starnes ordered his detail to leave prior to EOD defusing the threat.

Brigade was furious and refused to add 152's third platoon or Starnes's name to the report. Starnes's platoon sergeant demanded that the detail stay in place, but the lieutenant ordered the platoon to leave, and he was able to make it just in time to Camp Ramadi's dining facility for the lunch meal, leaving the EOD team without protection.

THE PIT

Many in the insurgency lived in Ar Ramadi, and we knew it. Insurgents were working diligently to turn the people's attitude and trust against coalition forces, and that included the Iraqi police. Local insurgents were spreading rumors that marines had recently kidnapped a young Iraqi girl. This created a public panic and later a demonstration at the South Area Ramadi Police Station known to coalition as SARS. I did not believe the rumor. Marines were not assigned to or patrolled in this section of Ramadi. To me, the story did not seem to add up.

An army master sergeant Jeff Anrich with the 152nd had recently took responsibility at SARS with Fourth Platoon. A few squads from the First Cav were running the station, but newly trained IPs were to be assigned to the station, so additional 152nd soldiers and additional supplies were needed at the station. After arriving, Anrich and his platoon were tasked to check into the rumored kidnapping and to calm tensions that were growing in this section of southern Ramadi.

Jeff's platoon was known as the Pit Bulls, and his police station was known as the Pit. And SARS was definitely a pit. The station was located in the northern section of Ramadi's highest populated area with dozens of apartments and housing complexes lined perfectly along dusty city streets and narrow alleys. Many of the police assigned to the Pit were uncomfortable working there. The area was dangerous, and the station was very shorthanded. But Jeff was soon to change things at the Pit.

The Pit was a vital station. It was to destroy the insurgency's free travel of using small inner city roads, attempting to bypass the main routes of enemy supply lines. Our presence at the Pit also kept the insurgency from recruiting Ramadi's youth or kidnapping them.

The master sergeant was a great guy and affectionately known to me and the 152nd commander as Jeff. Jeff called Kentucky home but served in the Indiana Army National Guard.

Early one morning, as the station was getting ready to have roll call with the IPs, a small group of Iraqis gathered outside of the SARS's main gate. Jeff walked toward the station's sole entrance with only his pistol on his hip and his usual pair of dark Oakley sunglasses. The Iraqi police assigned to SARS knew Jeff as a very personable man but also a tough, well-trained, and very smart leader. He was a bulldog but had a very calm, easy, and simple way to lead. They knew things would soon smooth over with the gathering at the gate.

Jeff stepped out of the station's main gate, not showing any fear, and approached the locals who had gathered and demanded to know about the rumors of the young mysterious girl who was missing. They thought the missing girl was at the station.

Jeff had just over seventeen years in the army and was already mentioned to be on the promotion list to the honored rank of sergeant major. Earning the rank of sergeant major in under twenty years is considered record time for any soldier in any specialty or job. Jeff was a career infantryman, a paratrooper, and a great soldier, well deserving of the promotion in my mind. With his interpreter relaying every word, Jeff asked for the village leader herding the small mob at the station. An older Iraqi man stepped up, visibly concerned about the accusations of a young Iraqi female detained and possibly harmed by marines in his village. Teenage girls were very protective in Iraq, rarely seen and not spoken about, specifically to foreigners.

"You can come right in," Jeff graciously explained to the group's leader. "You have full access to our facility, and you can bring others if you would like."

The Iraqi leader showed a sense of relief, and he entered the Pit's compound that was once an elementary school.

Jeff and I once discussed the 101st Airborne Division's Iraq disaster that had occurred a few years prior to the surge and our arrival to the combat zone. Four soldiers from the 101st decided to kidnap a local teenage Iraqi girl, rape the girl, and burn all evidence, evidence that included the girl and her entire family. The crime that happened in the small village of Mahmoudi, south of Baghdad, made international news and left an ugly scar on the 101st "Screaming Eagles" duty in Iraq. We did not want anything bad to happen with any of our soldiers, and proper leadership and supervision was the first element in combatting this.

To make the murder story worse, two months later, a pair of 101st soldiers were murdered in what was called "revenge for our sister who was dishonored by a soldier of the same division." The local insurgency formed a well-planned operation to lure leadership away from a patrol, then kidnap and murder two young Americans that dawned the Screaming Eagles' 101st unit insignia patch. This murder was based off the age-old principle found in Babylonian law of an "eye for an eye."

If it were not for the Mahmoudi kidnapping and murders, the two young soldiers could possibly be alive today, spending time with their family and friends.

The elder Iraqi was just as nervous as the IPs and Americans who were assigned to the station. Any wrong actions could result in disaster. The village leader slowly walked in, and the master sergeant showed respect with top-notch customs and courtesy.

"The key to the city is yours." The master sergeant laughed and put his right arm on the shoulder of the Iraqi, a show of friendliness and admiration in the Middle East. This eased the mind of the worried Iraqi, as well as the villagers who had gathered in the street.

Jeff's station did not cover much ground, and it did not take long for the elder's walk through. Ten minutes into the tour, the village leader, who was usually the oldest male of a village, strolled out of the compound as if he just left Willie Wonka's chocolate factory. The

Iraqi elder and Jeff were both laughing, shaking hands, a few slaps on the back…and peace was restored to the area that fell under SARS's responsibility.

Word of the Iraqi mob soon made its way to the brigade head-quarters at Camp Ramadi, and a call came to the SARS's communications room.

"Find the village leadership and drive them to our headquarters now!" was the message to Jeff from our higher command's operation cell.

"No need to worry. It has been taken care of, Cyclone 4-1 out," was the official reply from Jeff.

Headquarters demanded the order once again, but Jeff calmly relayed the same response.

Headquarters saw the morning's unrest of twenty-five or thirty locals who had gathered at the police station from above. The brigade owned several unmanned aerial aircraft, and the UAV gave perfect video of the unrest. The footage was sent immediately to the operations' cell but took sixty minutes to get a significant act report, better known as a SigAct, to reach the brigade commander. By the time the paperwork was compiled and completed, secure email delivered and collected, and once a liaison officer received the report in order for him to brief the nature of the cause or SigAct, decisions were then made. However, Jeff fixed this situation faster than a staff officer could relay the report.

"Have Cyclone 4-1 report to brigade now!" was the next order.

Jeff managed to show up at brigade headquarters later that day. The task to move from SARS to headquarters was not simple, safe, or easy to do. A detail of four armored trucks must be scrounged up. At least one dozen troops had to be assembled for the move that was only three miles from Camp Ramadi. A pre-mission brief had to be delivered, and the tactical move was rolled out on one of the most feared back roads of Ramadi. The trek was slow and careful, very slow. Most of the homes between SARS and Camp Ramadi had cinder block fences, difficult for even our gunners atop of our Hummers to view over. Jeff made sure there were plenty of bags of candy to toss over walls for kids to snatch and run off with. The kids simply treasured the sweets delivered by soldiers patrolling by. The bags of treats had to be hard candy; chocolate would melt. After several trips through the neighborhoods to or from SARS, when children could hear the roar of Hummers easing up the dusty and narrow roads, they would peer out of gate openings and holes in fence walls. Some kids would struggle to climb upon cinder block fences to get a rare glimpse of the Americans and perhaps receive a small bag of candy tossed from the gun trucks. Parents could be seen in doorways, cautious but curious of the convoy's mysterious visitors in their neighborhood. There were not bullets screaming from machine guns. But candy was being tossed to their children from Americans in armored trucks. This was something the local Iraqis had never witnessed. Most smiled as we convoyed past. Some could only glance from the corners of windows.

This was Jeff's way of earning trust with the locals. "They are nice" is what he wanted the locals to think as he and his men drove back and forth to man and run the station.

But at brigade, Jeff was voiced, "Why didn't you follow orders?"

The operations officer demanded several times to the calm and relaxed master sergeant, still covered with a fine dusting from the convoy to brigade headquarters.

"The problem was fixed," explained the master sergeant.

Several moments passed.

The chief relaxed and said, "Just don't ever do that again, Anrich."

"You mean don't ever fix problems?"

The brigade commander was within earshot of this conversation. He was troubled but pleased. He walked out of his office and said good job to Jeff. And much like Jeff putting his hand on the Iraqi village leader's shoulder, the brigade commander smacked Jeff on the back and just walked on. He knew the master sergeant was right but did not want to slam his staff for going by the book. Everyone learned a few things that day to include brigade staff of how things worked at the police stations and just how Jeff operated.

STATION LIFE

E very day was a challenge with the Iraqi police. And every day was something different, odd, or strange. One police station chief near Fallujah shot three of his subordinate policemen in their legs because they did not move out of his way quick enough. The station chief was later punished. The chiefs' penalty was thirty days paid administrative leave, pay each policeman twenty thousand dinar, roughly three hundred US dollars, and apologize to the family of the victims. Strangely, the station's chief was treated as a hero from most of the IPs at the station. Possibly treated a hero because the other IPs did not want to be the chief's next victim.

Each station's police chief was different, different in their own Iraqi way. Most were corrupt; it seemed that they would not be in their position if they were not corrupt. Kickbacks, bribes, and favors, it was an Iraqi way of doing business, and we could not change that fact in any way. Some police chiefs were possibly close to the insurgency or a certain insurgency cell. We had been told that a few police chiefs would have insurgent leaders invited into police station to discuss business, drink chai, and talk politics. Prior to our arrival in Ramadi, a police chief near Ramadi worked a *deal* with a local crew of insurgents. The deal was that each entity would simply leave each other alone. "You go your way and let us go ours" basically. The police station chief later changed his mind on the deal, he did not like certain ways the insurgents were acting in his area, and he voiced his change of heart publicly. Three days later, the police chief was dead. A car bomb slaughtered the chief and his driver while sitting in his vehicle. Three policemen from his station were seriously injured during the attack. The blast also wounded several of the chief's staff that were standing nearby. The attack happened right in front of his home as most of his family watched from the chief's front yard.

Some police station chiefs had several wives and a small mob of children. But multiple wives really did not seem to bother any of us who worked with the IPs. But it was, at times, hard to trust the senior leadership of the stations due to their well-known crooked ways of the country. The Iraqi way to get promoted or move up in the world was done through family members or bribes, but usually it was both. That is just how it was, and we could not change it and did not want to change anything. Our senior leaders pushed us to break the Iraqis away from bribes, payoffs, and corporal punishment, but we couldn't. Changing the Iraqi way was an impossible task.

But changing the fact that police station leaders were making deals or arrangements with the insurgency was not okay with us. That was the one Iraqi custom we would not accept, and the Ready First would not tolerate in any way.

Some Iraqi policemen knew where to patrol and where not to. Some knew where the hot spots were in Ramadi, they knew where deals have been made, and they knew where certain family lived that required special protection. Protection could be managed regardless of what side of the fence they sat on regarding terrorism and the insurgency. Family is very important to Iraqis, and a bribe thrown in can go very far.

We learned to spot an IP that was shady, just by body language and how they simply acted. Some were sympathetic or perhaps horrified by the insurgency. We had to be careful, yet trust the IPs.

We always knew something was wrong when the Iraqi radios in our 152nd Tactical Operations Center, better known as a TOC, went crazy with Arabic chatter and yelling. It was only a short matter of time that the brigade's deputy would call us up. Lieutenant Colonel Lechner would let the unit that supported the troubled area know what was going on, and he was always in the heat of every moment in what was his passion for success, Ramadi. Most panic calls like this one that arrived involved a large explosion or multiple explosions with plenty of gunfire. In Ramadi, there was always small arms gunfire after explosions. The headquarters for the 152nd was within easy view of the west side of Ramadi. With a good set of binoculars while standing on a large shipping container, most of the city could be seen. And the enemy could see us just as well. It reminded me of a bad marriage. Both parties could be seen and heard but hated each other and wanted the other to leave.

Large explosives were a constant threat and worry for us operating in and around Ar Ramadi. The province was known as an artillery and ordinance production and storage area, and large munitions were all over the place. Former Iraqi soldiers still living in the area were good with handling them and tampering with them, easily able to create IEDs to harm coalition convoys rolling by. For most men in Ar Ramadi, defusing a homemade bomb was as easy as changing a spark plug on a lawnmower. Munition dump sites were everywhere, and having a load of shells in your home was not out of the ordinary in Ramadi. Making booby traps and roadside bombs were simple; the difficult part was not getting caught setting them out on a road at night. We had plenty of eyes on the roads, observation posts, and snipers on rooftops and aircraft. Videos of how insurgents laid explosives on roadsides were sent out to units to watch and learn enemy tactics. We could see how they snuck up on roads from ditches or jumped out of vehicles to lay explosives down and then cover with a box or bury with sand or possibly cover the IED with a dead fox or jackal. In one aerial video released by our brigade's intelligence center, a group of six Iraqis were standing next to what appeared to be a stalled vehicle. The hood was up, and the group was gathered around the engine compartment. Moments later, all but one in the group dashed to the edge of the road, carefully laid down three large artillery shells, hooked up a few wires, and then ran back to the disabled car. Everything looked right, but the leader who stayed back with the car was visibly upset in the scratchy video as aviators discussed what was going on from their attack helicopter intercom system. The leader stomped over to the roadside explosive, adjusted a few things, checked a few wires, and stormed back to the men who remained at the car. He shook his fist at the men, then yelled and screamed at the insurgents-in-training. Just then a few rounds were fired from the helicopter, and the group bolted south of the truck along a dirt road. They jumped into a ditch about a hundred yards away, but little did they know, the helicopter had infrared night vision and fired a few more shots near their position. The group took off again, running for dear life as the sound of helicopter blades neared. The group managed to reach a truck that clearly had weapons mounted in the back, and the pilots were ordered to destroy the threat.

Setting a roadside bomb was easy in the cities. A bomb-setter could dash between buildings and not be detected by coalition forces during nightfall. The locals usually knew when they were laid out and could avoid them with ease. Locals avoiding an area was one indicator that something was wrong, alerting convoys rolling into a town or farming community that something was wrong. Silence was deadly, and the absence of pedestrians or closed stores were sure trouble.

Many attacks and roadside explosives were set from a hot spot in Tameem, near the White Apartments. The five-story apartment complex sat at center stage in Tameem, and the main doors to the complex were just twenty yards north of Route Michigan. Route Michigan ran east and west and was the main highway into Ramadi, but Michigan was barred from coalition travel. This was one of the most dangerous roads for Americans to convoy throughout the entire Iraqi theater. Route Michigan had been labeled *red* and unsafe for coalition travel, and the route's status wasn't looking to change in any way soon. It was too dangerous. The locals were even afraid of the deadly road that ran eastward of Ar Ramadi toward Fallujah. It was difficult for us to admit we could not travel eastbound through Ramadi on Route Michigan, and that its status was *red*, but the route was strictly forbidden for our passage.

I could not figure out why the White Apartments were called the White Apartments. The apartments actually had an odd yellowish, mustard color. But to us, they were called the White Apartments. The IPs also called this complex in the center of deadly Tameem the White Apartments.

An American Abrams tank, tipping the scale at a monstrous seventy-two tons, was lifted off the ground and flipped over after activating a devastating pressure plate early January on the far east side of Tameem. The tank veered off Michigan on a side road that wasn't cleared for travel. The mistake was deadly for the crew. No one survived the lethal and destructive pressure plate explosion that dreadful morning. That's how powerful some of the IEDs were in this area, able to lift an Abrams off the ground. Hummers activating a pressure plate packed with explosives were known to simply vanish due to the explosion.

I was told the Abrams crew became disoriented and traveled on an unauthorized road. The deadly mishap was taken very hard by the brigade on Camp Ramadi that day.

When well-planned and lethal complex attacks hit a convoy on Michigan, they were always very brutal. A few rounds shot from a rooftop on the right usually meant a large-scale attack followed from the near left. A quick response team could be hit once rolling in to recover damaged vehicles and gathering soldiers and marines injured or killed during an attack. Michigan's Tameem area was a horrible area to be at.

Civilians kept clear of where the devices were laid. They knew just how much power was in them and what they could do. Locals were terrified to contact the IPs of IEDs. Disrupting the insurgency's destruction was dangerous and deadly. Insurgents would not only go after civilians who got in their way, but entire families would suffer as well.

Most hits against coalition came within eyeshot of the White Apartments, and that was why coalition forces wanted to establish an Iraqi police station to the west of the apartment complexes to control Tameem and Check Point Jones. This new IP station in Tameem was something the insurgents did not want to see built, and keeping a solid hold of the area was desperately needed by the insurgency.

CALL FOR HELP

Just after soldiers of the 152nd were finishing lunch at Camp Ramadi's dining hall, a call came over the radio. Trouble was in Tameem. This time, trouble was near the Al Anbar University, located on the far south side of Ar Ramadi and directly south of Tameem. The university could easily be seen from the new Tameem Police Station. Reports came in that insurgents were kidnapping college students on busses as they were leaving the college area.

Most of the 152nd were unaware the large university was even operating. The university had been closed for a while during the war. It still looked deserted to us with little or no signs of use for months. The university was usually still and quiet. We rarely bothered to notice it or even patrol the area due to the silence and lack of any type of movement at all.

Family members of the students who were being ordered from their busses were in pure panic. Most of the families had cell phones to call for help. Some families had children who scampered to the police station, begging the IPs for help.

The insurgents had developed a well-detailed plan. It was a plan that involved four cars, about twelve men, and a few AK-47s. The lead car pulled directly in front of the first busload of unexpected students with a pair of vehicles blocking each side of the bus. Once stopping the buses, cars edged up to each side of the buses displaying their weapons, faces masked, and dressed in black. Three insurgents quickly jumped on the bus of shocked students and ordered all to show identification. Most of the males were aged seventeen and eighteen, and being a student meant their families had money, money to pay for their release. Or worse, the hostages could be recruited to join the insurgent effort or be killed. Any problems meant certain death for the students, and torture was always included.

The plan went flawless. The insurgents trained, practiced, and skilled themselves for a simple, swift, and much-needed win at the university that day. They must have practiced this plan over and over and over, and it worked for the moment. Fourteen young men were taken from the buses at gunpoint. They were half in shock and half filled with complete fear. Insurgents in this province were completely savage and ruthless. We were told Tameem was an area that enemy leadership would vacation or go in hiding for a few weeks to lay low or meet others involved in the insurgent effort from all over the region without fear of capture or attack. Locals in Ramadi were terrified of the insurgency.

The Al Anbar province was an area that Saddam Hussein declared victory over America and coalition forces after the 1990-'91 Gulf War. On Fallujah's main street was where a close friend to the former president lived. Above the home had a large balcony that Saddam Hussein famously fired a rifle into the air following the Gulf War, smiling as he declared victory over the Americans who were now leaving Saudi Arabia. Saddam's state-owned newspapers and media claimed coalition forces had left in defeat. One of our 152nd squad leaders claimed he had snuck onto the same balcony that Saddam declared victory, proudly boasting, "I shit on that balcony when we arrived in theater!"

Next for the insurgents was transporting the student victims from the buses trapped at the gates of the university to Route Michigan that was only a few miles away. The caravan with the hostages was to meet up with their senior leadership who were anxiously waiting in the White Apartments. The main parking lot of the White Apartments faced south with a perfect view of the university. These senior insurgents wanted to keep eyes on during the kidnapping from the top floor of the apartment. The insurgency needed cash for its evil cause, and ransom money from families to bail out their loved ones could buy plenty of weapons, ammunition, food, and payroll. Fliers were recently found posted in Ramadi, Al-Qaeda was recruiting, and cash was needed.

But as the students were being ordered off the buses, word was quickly getting out of the student's kidnapping at the university. Families with children attending classes that day at the university were in total horror, and the people of Ramadi were looking to the police to save them.

Ar Ramadi was an area with little power, poor infrastructure, high unemployment, and scraggly public transportation, but word of trouble could spread as fast as wildfire. Cell phones were in every home and somehow always charged. A surprising seven million Iraqis were known to have cell phones in Iraq, and it was amazing that Iraqis could keep cell phones charged during times of little or no public power.

Without hesitation, IPs were loading trucks with their American trainers. Soldiers of the 152nd that were on Camp Ramadi quickly loaded gun trucks and headed to Ogden Gate, the south gate in and out of Camp Ramadi. Ogden was also the quickest port to Tameem from our camp.

Our company had a great spot to call home on Camp Ramadi. Our assigned wooden shacks were located on the southeast corner of the compound. This made easy and quick access to the camp's south gate and within a few minutes of Route Jones. The roundabout just south of Ogden Gate was the hub to Route Mobile, Route Michigan, and Route Jones. Once at Check Point Jones, we could get to all key points in the area quickly to include our valuable police stations scattered throughout the province. These key routes that spawned to and from Jones were wide, and the roads were very familiar to our unit at this point.

Insurgents hustled their hostages to the side of the road, then blindfolded each of the terrified students as classmates looked on in total fear from the bus windows. The hostages were then hurried into the kidnappers' staged cars along each side of the buses. Students who were ordered to stay on the bus could only watch in horror as their classmates were shoved into the running cars. Situations like this one meant the kidnapped men held at gunpoint would probably not return or not return as the same person. If the men would return to their homes, a permanent limp or shattered arm would leave the victim useless to work in his hometown or fight against the insurgency. Most who resisted joining the insurgency were killed. If ransoms were not paid, gruesome tortures followed that could last for several weeks. The cruelties were so horrific that surviving was impossible.

Two teams and my resupply gun trucks of the 152nd scurried out of Ogden Gate jumping south onto Route Jones that lead to the Al Hurriya Police Station, just southeast of the camp. Iraqi policemen were quickly mounting up in trucks with their AK-47s and stuffing as many magazines of ammunition as they possibly could into cargo pockets. The IPs had brand-new Ford diesel trucks. Each station were issued five or six of these well-built American machines to patrol with or respond to emergencies. Front seats of the police trucks were reserved for leadership, providing guidance and direction. Usually a few lieutenants or an IP captain rode in the cab. The station chief usually rode in a smaller American-made truck with thick armor welded onto each door for protection. As usual, the beds of the trucks were loaded with ten to twelve Iraqi policemen. Some IPs wore masks. The masks were not only intimidating but were a form of protection. If insurgents recognized a policeman's face, the IP or the IP's family could be tortured or slaughtered.

Once the 152nd pulled up to the station, a sense of panic was in the air. Iraqis were loaded in IP trucks. They were slapping the cab's roofs, screaming that they were ready to go. But the Al Hurriya Station police chief was not on duty that day. His assistant was temporarily in charge. His assistant was Major Ahmad Mohammad. Major Mohammad had been fired and removed from the station twice but always seemed to return to the station that served Al Hurriya. Relatives or local politicians were always allowing the major back into the station that watched over the southwest side of Ramadi. Many figured Major Mohammad had the insurgents in his back pocket or was taking bribes from them. Too often, the station would be attacked with small arms fire or mortars lobbed in from nearby, but the major would just so happen to not be on duty that day. He always hesitated on conducting patrols in the area, and this major was always inside the safe compound walls of the station, never near the main gate or inspecting gun towers. If coalition forces and IPs conducted a joint patrol and the major was around, it was guaranteed to be a short and quick trip. Not a shot would be fired, not a single arrest, even with recent intelligence proving insurgents were living in a certain house and guaranteed to be inside hiding, the place would be empty, and the search would quickly be over, and IP trucks would then head back to the station.

It was very frustrating. But every time that we were assured the major was gone for good, he would somehow return. Somehow.

Major Muhammad was a short man with a thick moustache. He always carried a radio and constantly had a worried look on his face each time the 152nd or any coalition patrol rolled in or by the station. Helicopters flying overhead would catch his attention, and the major always had a look on his face that he was taking mental notes of the times of flights, type of aircraft, and direction. He always wore a baseball cap. The hat was dark blue, and he never wore a traditional Iraqi headdress like most IPs did. Many thought the major was keeping away from Iraqi customs to throw off suspicions of his loyalties. He rarely made eye contact with anyone and always had his radio resting against his left cheek, even when he was not talking on it. The volume was always low, and he would keep the radio in the same spot all the time.

Once the 152nd convoy rolled into the station's compound, a large cloud of dust followed. The IPs were ready, and they were going to lead the way to the university to save the students trapped by the insurgents. That's how it worked. The 152nd were there to ensure the IPs were active, protected, and successful.

But Major Muhammad had other plans. He was ordering the station IPs to "stand down."

I quickly popped my head out of my gun truck door. "What is wrong?"

"We cannot go," the major hesitantly said and, of course, with his handheld radio pressed next to his left cheek. "I was just told the insurgents will kill us if we leave this compound but not harm Americans."

"Forget you," I screamed as translators repeated. "Load them up and get the IPs in the trucks. Time is ticking!"

"No! We must not go. We have been warned," the major repeated, looking around as if other IPs would concur with his commands.

"We will go without you and take care of this ourselves," I said as I turned to my truck, waving a visual command to get prepared to move out.

As the 152nd were ready to roll, the station chief's truck and security detail was entering the gate. He knew what was going on at the university. He already had a plan to get to the students; he was ready.

Colonel Yasin Kaddam had been in command at the station for just over two years. The colonel had made enormous improvements to the station and provided a much better way of life for the local Iraqis in his area of responsibility. And the colonel wanted to keep it that way.

Colonel Kaddam was always serious and extremely focused. He always carried a clipboard with bright-yellow papers, but he never wore a hat or *kufiyah* for some unknown reason. He always had a clean perfectly pressed Iraqi police uniform and was very proud of it. His staff jumped at his every command, and the IPs were loyal to the colonel. He was completely diplomatic and always polite to Americans who assisted with his needs to ensure a safe and productive station to live and work at.

As the colonel directed IPs to move out of the compound, Major Muhammad turned and walked away. He later climbed in an IP truck, but not many knew the major was in the convoy that was rolling out. The 152nd didn't want him there. He was a threat to our security, and he had the radio that could possibly be used to tell actions, locations, and intent of the security detail to the hostage takers.

"We have got to get to the university!" I relayed to Colonel Kaddam as his truck passed mine.

The colonel did not respond, and he did not need to. Just the nod of the colonel's head and firm grip on the truck door explained his intent. The convoy rumbled down the station's narrow road that was only one hundred meters from Check Point Jones, then arced the roundabout onto Route Michigan. Locals could be seen peeking through doorways and windows, braving the dust cloud and roar of the convoy's diesel engines charging toward the university. They had to get a peak of what could be a fierce battle that was within eyeshot of their Iraqi homes.

Being from Indiana and in the Indiana Army National Guard meant we were huge Colts fans. We were in Ramadi while the Indianapolis Colts won the Super Bowl.

Iraqi Police senior leader and a senior leader with the US Marines chat and drink tea one morning at the Husaybah Police Station. The Marines were based out of Fallujah, and also ran North TQ.

Our unit had sniper rifles as well as a few trained snipers. This photo was taken on Route Michigan, near the White Apartments.

This is me with my interpreter "Romeo". Not sure what his real name was, but Romeo was a great guy and friend. He warned me of the bounty placed on me by the Insurgency.

Marine Corps Major Megan McClung, Killed in Action
December 6, 2006 in Ramadi while on patrol. The Major was
the Ready First Public Affairs Officer and deeply involved
in the "Anbar Awakening". Megan always had a smile
on her face, and very kind to all.

Captain Travis Patriquin was known for his perfect Arabic
language, people skills, and keeping things simple. But
he was also known for his thick, Iraqi-style moustache.
Killed in action in Ramadi in December 2006.

A tribute to our sole fallen Soldier with the 152 during The Surge, Staff Sergeant Bradley King. We had a handful of usable trucks once arriving at Camp Ramadi, but our 152 mechanics brought our company from non-mission capable to running missions throughout Anbar within days after arriving in Ramadi. Sgt First Class Laddy is far right in photo.

This is Lt General Sean MacFarland.
As a Brigade Commander with the First Armor, he led the "Anbar Awakening" during "The Surge".

Myself with Captain Amanda Pendley at Fort Lewis Washington, she is an intelligence officer with the Indiana Army National Guard. I credit the intel community for saving many lives in Iraq. We deployed together to Iraq in 2010-2011. We remain friends to this day. Amanda speaks multiple languages and a brilliant intelligence officer.

This is me with the Habbaniyah Police Station Chief's oldest son. He was a good kid and loved to trade any type of item with Americans. We would spend time together every day.

FOILED GETAWAY

As the kidnapper's cars sped north with their cargo of abducted students and the small town of Tameem was coming into view, the small convoy prepared to link up with senior leadership who was waiting and watching the heist from the top floor of the White Apartments. The captors were planning to smuggle their victims to an Al-Qaeda safe place somewhere in the Al Anbar Province and hold them for a few days in a makeshift dungeon. Soon ransom demands would make its way to hostages' families. That is one of the tricks that the insurgency paid for its evil ways. This tactic was something that the world news seemed to not care about or report, but it happens, and events like this is how most of Al-Qaeda's funds are raised.

The blindfolded victims who were stuffed in their captors' cars sat silent in pure fear, unknown of their future as hostages. As Route Michigan came into view, the kidnappers began to see large dust clouds being kicked up by the charging convoy of IP trucks from the west. Soon, blue IP lights caught the attention of the lead driver of the northbound caravan. The Iraqi police were on their way, and when Iraqi police are heading someplace with lights and sirens blaring, US Forces were always nearby as well, trailing the white and blue IP trucks. Brigade staff on Camp Ramadi were watching as well by video from the air. UAVs circled the city day and night for the brigade. UAVs were mainly checking for enemy mortar teams operating in the area, or an IED team planting explosives on the side of a road that was known to be traveled on by coalition forces. The UAV images were surprisingly clear, and most of the aircraft could zero on items as small as a brick. Details could be spotted by technicians in the brigade headquarters, and reports were then sent to command staff. These reports were forwarded to combat units on the ground, and action was quickly taken.

The techs that manned the UAV footage at brigade were fascinating to watch. Something out of the unusual that the average soldier would consider nothing would spark their attention. Within seconds, the questioned item could be zoomed in with spectacular quality. These guys were great, and they could spot trouble better than a passing convoy with ease. These were unsung heroes, heroes that received little or no gratification. But I am assured, these UAV teams saved many, many lives during the war.

I was ordered to stage my four Humvees just east of Check Point Jones as our convoy of IP trucks and hummers continued past us and stormed down Route Michigan. I was to keep clear of the fight and assist with the resupply effort. Prior to leaving our headquarters shack, my team loaded thousands of rounds of ammunition, a few boxes of smoke grenades, several cases of water and grabbed all the first aid kits we could find for the trip that we really didn't know much about. We only knew people needed our help and quickly needed our help.

As the three black BMWs and a silver Mercedes approached Michigan from the university, the lead driver slowed as he neared the intersection, unsure of what to do as IP trucks could clearly be seen approaching.

The gunner of the IP convoy's lead truck zeroed his gunsight on the insurgent's lead car, and the policeman did what Iraqis like to do, the IP unloaded a few dozen rounds of ammunition toward the northbound insurgents' car, aiming for tires and the engine block. These well-placed rounds quickly disabled the lead car, the second IP truck joined in the firefight by directing bullets into the rear vehicle's tires. The lead BMW veered to the right after seeing incoming rounds, arriving at a violent and fierce rate that shredded each front tire as steam erupted from its bullet-ridden radiator. The convoy of IP trucks quickly had the upper hand with eight or nine policemen in the rear of each truck now firing madly. The insurgent's response was weak. They could only muster one rifle out of each passenger window with little effect against the IP barrage of gunfire. There was simply no match for the kidnappers against the IPs. Dust from the edge of the road provided the insurgent convoy a form of a dust screen as the IPs closed their distance from their targets by twenty yards, causing a slight pause of the IPs firepower. The lead BMW, with smoke barreling out of its engine compartment, somehow limped into the parking lot of the White Apartments and came to a sudden halt within a few feet of the apartment's front door.

Hobbling into the parking lot of the White Apartments was a deadly decision for the insurgent convoy, but the only safe haven at this point. They had no other place to turn with their wounded cars. Leadership from the apartments may have ordered the convoy into the parking lot, but they were sitting ducks as the IPs pulled to a stop in front of the White Apartment's parking lot entrance, blocking the kidnappers' only exit.

With smoke and dust kicking as high as fifteen feet, the insurgents abandoned their getaway cars in the parking lot and began running into the White Apartments. The insurgents' scurry into the White Apartments was comical. They were trying to drag a few of the hostages into the front doors of the apartment, but the blindfolded students just could not keep up. Several of the insurgents tripped during the frantic dash to safety, eventually releasing their hostages along the way. The kidnappers were in a panic making every effort to reach the safety of the front doors of the White Apartments as IPs began to close in, but the plan was quickly falling apart for the insurgency.

Trapped inside the White Apartments, locals informed us that over sixty insurgents were inside, keeping a close eye on the university as the kidnapping operation unfolded. Top floors of the White Apartments had a perfect view of the university, and an excellent view of Route Michigan and Check Point Jones. One apartment was used as an insurgent intelligence center. We later found out that this Intel office kept track of all coalition movement with great detail, specifically at Check Point Jones. This tracking included Iraq Police movement. Records were found detailing how many convoys rolled by per hour, how many fuel trucks were included in convoys per day, and what type of vehicles were in each convoy. Weapon systems mounted on vehicles of each convoy that strolled across Michigan or through Jones were recorded. The tracking was so detailed, records included the name of each unit on the roads. Maps of Ramadi's police stations were nailed to the room's walls, and photos of each station's chief were found as well.

As the chaos continued, people who resided at the White Apartments quickly ran for cover. Most ran down a side street to the north that took them to the marketplace of Tameem, seeking shelter with a relative, friend, or in a store. Some locals stuck in the White Apartments could only shut their windows, locked their doors, and huddle in closets with their families to avoid harm.

Two of the hostages managed to break away as the insurgents struggled to dash across the parking lot of the White Apartments, blindfolded with their hands bound with rope. The duo somehow were able to run away or perhaps were abandoned as IPs and Americans began to circle the complex, boxing and trapping the kidnappers and their leadership. With hands tied behind their backs and unable to see, the young Iraqi men managed to run toward a few parked cars and hid between them as gunfire was exchanged to and from the White Apartments. I noticed a few of the captors were left at the front steps of the White Apartments and sat in silence and shock. Sirens and loudspeakers plagued the neighborhood as the insurgents made their way to the apartment's rooftop, another deadly decision for the kidnappers, but their only decision available.

My resupply convoy of four gun trucks and a trailer continued to wait between Check Point Jones and the White Apartments, filled to the brim with ammunition and supplies. We were also tasked to block off civilian traffic from Check Point Jones heading east toward the fight at the apartments. We waved forward coalition trucks and armored vehicles from Camp Ramadi toward the apartments to join in the fight. The IP and American perimeter around the White Apartments continued to grow stronger and stronger by the minute. Our spot on Michigan was in perfect view of the fight, the best seats in the town.

From the apartment complex's fifth floor, the insurgent leader came up with a quick plan for a counterattack. He ordered his men to line up against the wall of the rooftop's edge and just start firing at the IPs and Americans below. It was not the best plan ever created by a militia, but at least it was a plan, a plan that would fail miserably.

Several insurgents on the rooftop did not have a chance during the skirmish and were killed immediately. The IPs had completely circled the complex, Americans were close by as well, and the entombed kidnappers were hit one by one. Several were sliced in half at the waist by the machine guns firing that were mounted to IP trucks. IPs who were known to be the station's best shots were focusing on enemy fighters peeking through windows or attempting to get a glance at the ground fighters from the roof. But the fight was clearly in favor of the IPs on the ground.

While I was staged near Check Point Jones, my main concern was, "Will the IPs run out of ammunition before we get there?" The IPs were heavily unloading on the kidnappers, and the insurgents were taking casualties at a rapid pace.

The battered and beaten insurgents had limited ammunition without a chance of any resupply effort, and being trapped equaled sure failure. Iraqi police on the ground returned fire with great accuracy under the watch of their own IP leadership, and the Americans continued to provide overwatch as we were told to do. The insurgent's return of fire soon became sporadic, a bit on the undisciplined side, and at times, some just took wild shots that didn't even fall near any of us on the ground. But this plan was their best and only hope at the time; they were trapped rats. IPs on the ground developed a fantastic perimeter and had perfect cover as armored vehicles rambled in to assist in the fight at the White Apartments.

Chunks of cement fell to the ground at the base of the apartment complex, and several windows were shattered during the fight. A few rounds went over the building, and I was not sure where they landed in the Tameem area. There were a few dozen apartment complexes and a small strip of stores that stood to the north of the White Apartments, but neither party seemed to care about this fact. Most the locals were hunkered down during this battle, not wanting to be hit by a stray bullet. Iraqis were accustomed to this inner city fighting, the war had been going since 2003, many of the Ar Ramadi children have grown up with this fighting and bloodshed as a part of their daily lives...nothing new to them at all. It was simply a way of life in Iraq, and something that could not be prevented it seemed. Most just hoped the war's effects would not happen near them or harm them or their family.

As the 152nd gun trucks edged closer to the IPs blasting away at the apartment building, several gunners atop the Hummers equipped with longer range machine guns opened fire with exact precision. Enemy gunners on rooftops were literally being sliced in half by the American .50 caliber rounds streaming in.

I was not far away, still on Route Michigan, in the lead hummer of the resupply convoy, facing east toward the White Apartments with a perfect view of the remarkable firefight at the base of the White Apartments. To my immediate left were a few Iraqi houses and an alley that ran northeast into the shopping district of Tameem that we had recently conducted the Tameem Sweep, also known as Operation Buttercup. The alley had my full attention as the fight surged to our direct front. We were in the danger area of a possible ambush being so close to the very dangerous Check Point Jones area. Over the last two months, we had had far too many close calls at this section on Route Michigan as we drove toward the dangerous roundabout.

While scanning the suspicious alley to my left, silhouettes appeared between two darkened buildings. This had me and my driver very worried.

Our orders were to stay on Route Michigan, approximately two hundred meters to the west of the White Apartments until called forward with supplies and medical transport if needed. But I requested

JB GARRISON

the push forward due to the strange activity in the alley to our north. It just did not seem right, and we had been sniped at from this area just several days prior.

"Cyclone 6, Cyclone 5, over," I called to Henton, who was positioned at the front and center of the fight ahead as rounds were exchanged between the two groups.

"Six, go."

"Permission to pull forward, threat to our extreme left between buildings," was my request.

"Granted," Henton stated.

"Five moving, out." And our supply convoy pulled forward to the White Apartments and a little closer to the fight.

The figures in the dark could have been kids trying to get a rare glimpse of Americans and a few gun trucks, or it could have been an RPG crew. We were not taking any chances with the safety of our truck crews and valuable cargo.

Once nearing the battle site, I led our detail to the south of the main effort securing the White Apartments. We were to double up as resupply and rear security for the remainder of the fight. As our convoy came to a halt, two IP trucks screamed west on Route Michigan, each with a handful of insurgents lying in the back, handcuffed and blindfolded. These captured insurgents were going straight to the Iraqi Police district headquarters and placed into custody. Another truck transported one injured IP, heading to Camp Ramadi with an obvious bullet wound to his leg. He was holding his left leg that was covered in bloodied bandages, and several IPs were by his side for the ride.

It was clear the IPs had the advantage in the fight and obviously had the upper hand. The kidnappers trapped themselves atop of the apartment complex and were sitting ducks. Winning this fight was a matter of time as the IPs held a tight perimeter around the apartment building and destroyed the desperate kidnappers with ease one-by-one.

Once the IPs that had contained the White Apartments saw that our convoy was assisting in the fight with fresh supplies, ammunition boxes quickly disappeared from the trucks, and cracked open in a flash. IPs loaded their arms with as much ammo as they could possibly grab and ran as fast as they could run to the frontline of the fight. The ammunition simply vanished in front of our very eyes, and the IPs wanted more. As ammo was being distributed to the prone IPs, several insurgents could no longer handle the firefight and surrendered, perhaps conceding after viewing the additional ammunition arrive.

They surrendered and looked in shock. They could not handle the barrage of firepower any longer.

As the kidnappers were quickly being killed one by one on the apartment's rooftop, a trio of terrified hostages that were earlier hustled into the complex bolted out of the complex's main door to be collected by a squad of IPs. This collection team verified that any fleeing hostages were in fact one of the students snatched from the buses earlier that day and not an insurgent posing as a freed captive. The rescued hostages were freed of their blindfolds and restraints, and offered water as the fight continued.

Between two Bradleys, an Iraqi boy was sitting in an Iraqi police truck. The boy only seemed eight years old, and he was visibly frightened, shaking with fear. I was worried that the boy was detained as an Insurgent. But gladly, I was wrong. He was trapped in the middle of the fight on his way home from school, and a team of IPs ordered him into one of their IP trucks for protection. He said his family lived in one of the houses to the east of the White Apartments, and he wanted to go home. Our goal was to get him home by nightfall, but there was no way to inform the boy's family that he was safe until the fight was over.

I noticed Captain Henton was joining in the fight. Our company commander remained on the front line with his 152nd soldiers. To my immediate left, standing carelessly next to a few Bradleys was the DCO, Lieutenant Colonel Lechner. But to my surprise was Colonel MacFarland standing to the DCO's right, both watching the battle in the parking lot of the White Apartments. The duo orchestrated the "Anbar Awakening" and did not want to miss this battle at the apartments. Winning the fight at hand was close to their hearts, and winning was their pure passion. I was in awe. These men put everything on the line, months ago, and craved a huge win and desperately needed a solid win against the insurgency.

As the sun was starting to set over the White Apartments, a *lull* in the battle began, and the area soon became quiet, but the quiet was an earie kind of quiet. Policemen quickly reorganized during the odd silence, spread out fresh ammunition to front-line IPs, while they carefully kept full attention to the threat at hand.

The insurgents were also trying to reorganize as darkness arrived, but their numbers were quickly dwindling due to being killed or wounded during the battle. A second desperate rooftop attack broke the odd silence just as darkness set over the apartment's courtyard, but the attack did not help the insurgents' desperate plight. Iraqi police were spread out along all sides of the complex and were beginning a flanking position to the east of the apartment complex. A violent attack was in work against the few remaining insurgents trapped in the White Apartments. Several additional Bradly Fighting Vehicles arrived from Camp Ramadi and coalition forces overwhelmingly had the upper hand over the insurgents surrounded in the apartment complex. Several IP trucks were instructed to drive back and forth in front of the White Apartment's main door, with their red and blue lights brightening up the area. Two of the trucks had loudspeakers, and the IPs were chanting and yelling in Arabic.

I asked a translator what they were yelling, and he said, "The IPs are calling them chicken asses and to come out and fight...or surrender."

Illumination rounds exploded over the city from Camp Ramadi's "Glory's Guns" artillery battalion. Squad leaders from the 152nd occasionally fired flairs from grenade launchers between the camp's high-flying illumination rounds, providing a lit battlefield for all to view. One illumination round fired from Camp Ramadi drifted into the garage of an Iraqi's home to the east of the apartments. I was surprised to see the owner of the house just walk out of the front door of the home with a rug and put out the fire as if it was nothing. Once the flames were put out, he casually strolled back in the house.

Two hours after nightfall, only a few shots were exchanged between the insurgents and our coalition effort that surrounded the apartments. The insurgents must have been reduced to just a few rounds of ammunition and knew that their time was running out in the fight. The last few insurgents that managed to survive surrendered to IP sweep teams. IPs began foot patrolling around the complex as illumination flairs continued to pop over the White Apartments. The fight was over.

Shortly after midnight, life returned to normal for the people who called the White Apartments home. Lamps were turned back on, window blockades were removed, and the people went back to doing whatever they would usually do. Sadly, war was a normal way of life for the Iraqi People in Ar Ramadi.

As a bizarre silence fell over the town of Tameem and the smoke cleared, Colonel Kaddam hopped into an IP truck with a squad of his policemen and drove up to the front door of the White Apartments. The colonel grabbed his bullhorn and asked the people of the White Apartments if they wanted rouge insurgents in their complex and neighborhoods. Or safety with his IPs? He made it clear to the residents of the White Apartments it was up to them to bring freedom back to their neighborhood and eventually the city of Ar Ramadi. The colonel was right, and the answer was clear to all in the area, life would be better without the Insurgency.

IP trucks continued to slowly circle the apartments, eager to snatch an insurgent attempting to scamper for safety from the White Apartments. Insurgents that did manage to survive and surrender were gathered with dignity, provided water and safety. They were disarmed as IPs ordered the Insurgents to approach with their arms stretched to the sky. Most were begging for help and seemed in shock from the fierce battle that the IPs and Americans had blasted at them with full force. Loudspeakers were blaring instructions to surrender, sirens lit up the night, and policemen could be seen proudly waving their AK-47s in the air in celebration. This was a huge victory for the

IPs and the people in the area who knew the IPs easily had control over the city and saved the hostages from an unsure future. Soon, the complex was cleared, apartment by apartment, room by room. Remarkably, we were told that there were no locals injured or killed in the fight at the apartments that night. And we began plans to move back to Camp Ramadi.

THE SMOKE CLEARS

nitial reports from Ready First Battalion and Brigade Intelligence offices were shocking. With severe enemy losses and injuries from the battle that erupted at the White Apartments, insurgent leadership were forced to drastically adjust plans to fight and operate in the Al Anbar Province. Coalition forces had twenty-eight confirmed kills that evening during the battle at the White Apartments, but it was probably more. Twenty-two were reported as captured enemy prisoners of war. Many were injured to a point that they would not survive battle wounds or be functional to fight another day. Reports also claimed over twenty insurgents were seen crossing the nearby Tameem Canal, a waterway that spurred from the Euphrates River that eventually feeds nearby Lake Habbaniyah. The grassy canal that ran southeast of the White Apartments was used as a passageway for the few insurgents who were able to retreat that night. Enemy squads changed from eleven-man teams to three-man teams according to intelligence reports and later changed to two-man teams. This foiled attack proved costly for anti-coalition forces working in the area, and the fight tilted the public's favorable opinion in our direction.

The insurgency suffered major losses that evening at the White Apartments, but the most damage was their broken relationship with the Iraqi people in the province. The local Iraqis no longer tolerated the Insurgency and refused to bow to their control. Colonel Khaleed's leadership, diplomacy, and policing following the attack against the people of Ramadi turned to become Coalition Force's best weapon. IPs storming right into the heart of the battle to confront the enemy, showing protection and safety for the community.

All roads in Ramadi and coalition checkpoints following the battle of the White Apartments quickly became peaceful and quiet, almost too quiet at times. Driving on Route Michigan or Route Jones was strange and a bizarre type of strange. It seemed as the quiet after the storm. The brigade was now able to convoy with Abrams tanks and Bradleys safely through Check Point Jones, strengthening "Old Ironsides" grip in the region. IPs patrolled Ramadi with ease, and the enemy threat was now sharply minimized. This was a sight I thought I would not see during our unit's tenure in the Iraqi theater.

Several stores in the Tameem marketplaces reopened, and existing stores began to keep longer hours the week following the battle that erupted without warning in front of the White Apartments that January afternoon. The usual potshots didn't strike coalition vehicles crossing the Euphrates River into Ramadi or passing by the old Ramadi Glass Factory just north of Check Point Jones. An observation post was manned at Check Point Jones and another between TIPS and Route Michigan, a spot where machine gun fire was once easily sprayed at passing American convoys and rocket propelled grenades were chucked at coalition convoys just about every night.

Our third platoon gathered items to donate to a local elementary school in Tameem. We wanted the local IPs to go with us, and they wanted to join us. It was a win-win for Americans and the local policemen. The schools had very little as far as supplies and materials for the children, and schoolteachers and school leaders accepted the items as if they were gold. The treasures donated to the school was a huge hit, and we knew by the many smiles and thanks from the kids. Many have only heard of Americans and American cultures. Some only knew of Americans that passed by their homes in convoys stirring dust in heavily-armored machines that seemed as colossal monsters roaring through neighborhoods with machine guns mounted, stopping for nothing. Stopping for nothing but a fight. But those days seemed over.

BATTLE OF THE WHITE APARTMENTS

One sergeant from third platoon, Justin Betnar, read from a book to a group of thirty wide-eyed Iraqi schoolchildren during a book giveaway as an interpreter carefully translated. It seemed as if the Iraqi children did not know that Americans owned a *soft* side. Only rumors and tales of the American wild west, pistols on our hips, tumbleweeds rolling down dusty streets. Justin stood just over six-foot-tall and had brushy red hair. He had a very light complexion, and that kept the kids' full attention as they sat in pure awe.

The most surprising effect from the recent coalition victory was the many pedestrian bridge crossings that stretched over Route Michigan. Once used as enemy battle positions, the crossways were now painted a light blue with green flowers running up and down the stairwells. Route Michigan was once too dangerous for pedestrians to walk near and once had very little vehicle traffic. It was incredible to see the roads used once again.

Police assigned to the Tameem station were now conducting foot patrols through the apartments without fear or any trouble, handing out candy to kids as they played in courtyards, and walked home from school without the fear of the insurgency kidnapping them. The locals enjoyed seeing the police monitoring the area and felt safe for the first time in many years.

TAKE TWO

Exactly one week following the battle of the White Apartments that strangled the enemy's might in Anbar, trouble stirred once again at Ramadi University's entrance. Insurgents, wanting desperately to rebound from their crushing defeat one week prior, again cornered a bus returning to the Tameem area with a few dozen students aboard. Similar to the plan that had failed one week earlier. The insurgency was now desperate in Ramadi, and it clearly showed. UAVs locked onto two buses cornered at the university's entrance following calls for help.

I knew how serious this was when an Air Force F-15 buzzed the southeast side of Camp Ramadi as 152nd trucks were staging to exit Camp Ramadi's Ogden Gate. Everyone knew just where the pilot was heading, to rattle the Tameem area. As the F-15 zipped over our heads, the pilot banked east and dipped lower, kicking in his jet's afterburners over the small Tameem neighborhood and quickly disappeared into the clear blue skies of western Iraq.

I was sure that the F-15 was only there for presence, and that was perfectly fine with me. When the powerful bird blasted over the many Tameem high-rises to rattle rooftops, I am very sure the pilot had everyone's full attention that coalition forces meant serious business. I am not sure who contacted the air force or requested the pilot buzz the neighborhood, but it was incredibly impressive and a huge attention-getter. It was a good feeling knowing that the air force would be close by and providing air cover while we were heading back to Tameem with the locals in distress once again.

The pilot banked high and bolted far south and out of our sights only to return. The pilot spotted the busses boxed in near the university and streaked directly over the heads of the insurgents who were standing in complete fear in the roadway. The blast deafened the kidnappers as they attempted to cover their ears with their hands while dust and small rocks pelted their skin, hurling a few to the side of the road.

My resupply convoy departed Ogden Gate and roared toward Check Point Jones as fast as we could possibly go, then stormed east on Route Mobile to stage near the White Apartments. IPs from Ramadi's Main District Station had also been alerted and were heading south for another rendezvous with the insurgents.

Once Third Platoon and a few additional 152nd trucks reached the Al Hurriya Station, Major Muhammad was near the station's front gate. He was not allowing the Al Hurriya police to leave the compound. Trucks were loaded with IPs, weapons were locked and loaded, but the major was refusing to let them leave the compound.

"We have been told the Insurgents would shoot only us if we responded to another crisis," he yelled over and over.

My convoy stopped just east of Check Point Jones to link up with the Al Hurriya IPs, waiting for their convoy to exit the compound. But we could only watch the trucks as they idled in the parking lot of the station. I could see Major Muhammad nodding his head back and forth.

Finally, I radioed, "We'll leave without them. Forget it!"

My frustration with Muhammad was beyond control.

Just then, Colonel Kaddam arrived at his station in his blue IP truck, and the chief's security detail was not far behind. The colonel had his handheld radio and knew exactly what was happening at the university. He overruled his deputy's commands, and the convoy bolted east, once again toward the nearby university, ready for a rematch. At this point, our usual routine or protocol of traveling on Route Jones was not followed in any way. There was not a convoy brief, no alternate route, and no safety plan. We wanted to get there and get there quickly. Rules and standards were out the window, and we just flew down the road toward the frantic calls for help.

The people of Al Hurriya area knew we meant business as a large dust storm kicked up from the rampant IP convoy. I noticed each house or business had curtains drawn, but an occasional pair of eyes could be seen peeking out of windows along the way.

From the start, the second kidnapping attempt failed in every way for the insurgents. The students who were ordered to exit the buses simply refused to walk off. And as sirens screamed from the Al Hurriya Police Station toward the university, the insurgents did just as a week earlier, headed north toward Route Michigan, but this time, without hostages.

Much like a week earlier, the two forces clashed in front of the White Apartments, and the so-called hostage takers hurried into the parking lot of the apartment building. IP bullets were fiercely hurled their way, striking cars, leaving a trail of bullets zipping across the ground as if chasing the insurgents dashing into the apartment's main doors. But the fight was no match for the frantic insurgents. With a swift and violent attack by the IPs, with Americans in tow to support, the insurgent force took another heavy loss. Many ran off into the neighboring apartment complexes. Some tried to fight back, but it was over quickly and very bloody. The combined effort of IPs with American support destroyed what remained of the enemy. Locals watched from afar as the IPs soundly defeated the Insurgent's final attempt to create terror in their city.

IPs from other stations responding to the call captured most of the fleeing insurgents. They were detained and hauled off to the main station in tears.

My resupply convoy idling at Check Point Jones pushed east to the White Apartments, observing the fight that mirrored the January 10 battle one week ago. Within minutes, my resupply convoy staged south of the coalition's stronghold as we did the week prior and again sat as rear security with no threat in sight.

The police had the insurgents once again trapped at the White Apartments but far less of a battle this evening than a week earlier. A pair of insurgents had been captured in the parking lot. They were quickly whisked away in the back of an Iraqi police truck, sirens blaring. A few stayed to fight it out that managed to make it to the rooftop of the White Apartments, but the IPs quickly killed off the remaining enemy that chose to fight. It was no match at all.

Iraqi policemen called out to any remaining trapped insurgents to surrender and to not put the lives and well-being of families who lived in the White Apartments at risk. As dusk fell on the Tameem area, several dedicated Al-Qaeda faithful refused to surrender. But after a few hours, several surrendered to IPs staged in the parking lot. With arms stretched up high, the few who did surrender were searched for weapons and offered water and safety from the fight. The battle was over for them, and a team of IPs brought the exhausted and distraught prisoners to the main station for processing.

Some had been recruited into the insurgency by force. Some had joined for employment to simply feed their family. These Iraqis would be processed and eventually returned to civilian life if they swore to not return to the insurgency.

Flares lit the neighborhood as night fell on the west side of Ar Ramadi, and it became obvious that the few remaining insurgents on the top floors were not going to surrender. A few squads of policemen were dispatched into the main entryway of the White Apartments just before midnight, and the remaining insurgents were escorted at gunpoint out of the apartment complex, hustled into police trucks, and swept off to the main police station for detainee processing. The fight was officially over around ten that night.

Of course, Colonel MacFarland and his deputy Lieutenant Colonel Lechner were there in the fight. The pair were very pleased with the second pounding of an insurgent attack against the people of the area.

At midnight, leadership was drawing down on the number of American soldiers we had on ground at the base of the White Apartments. The danger and threat level was no longer serious, and moving out was planned and organized. With the fight over, we could get back to Camp Ramadi, and the locals could get back to bed and get ready for another Tameem day in the morning.

I was asked to escort a pair of ASVs from Lieutenant Bennick's platoon back to Camp Ramadi. We were still required to travel with a minimum of four vehicles outside of the perimeter of the camp, and security always remained top priority, mainly moving in and around Tameem and Check Point Jones at night.

As our convoy lined up to head west back to Camp Ramadi, my Hummer crew took the rear security spot. Rear security did not mean it was the safest spot. It was the danger zone. I dreaded rear convoy security but gladly accepted it without hesitation. As company executive officer, that was *my* dangerous position. But with the experienced truck crew that I was heading back to Camp Ramadi with, I did not worry much at all. This crew was top-notch and feared nothing in any way. My gunner was quick with the trigger and knew the number 1 rule to combat ambush, "If ambushed, you have the rest of your life to survive it." We were not far from home, and a short distance from the safe confines of Camp Ramadi's Ogden Gate.

Strolling up to Ogden Gate was always a welcoming view. This meant you survived another day in deadly Anbar. My family worried about me in Iraq, but I gave little details. They did not even know I was running convoys along some of the deadliest roads in the world. I didn't tell them, not even my dad. They didn't need to know.

As we continued west on Route Michigan on that dark and dusty night, I watched the White Apartments disappear from my Hummer's rearview mirror as a few illumination rounds brightened the parking lot and neighboring areas.

With a smile, I sent a radio message to our company headquarters operations shack, "Cyclone-1, this is Cyclone-5. Heading to Ogden Gate. Four VICS, twelve PAX. Approaching Check Point Jones, over."

"Cyclone-5, good copy, over."

"Five out."

Just as the conversation with the 152nd operations shack ended, our gun truck came to a crashing halt, jarring the crew of five, sending me into near shock.

"What happened? What did we hit?" I asked through the Hummer's intercom system, looking into the dark and dust that had been kicked up by the convoy's sudden standstill.

What was that? I thought we had hit the roundabout's fountain, but I was wrong. I looked to the front of our gun truck as a large cloud of dust settled to see one of TB's ASV just a few inches in front of our hummer and motionless. We rear-ended the machine for some reason. The ASV was stalled without power, no lights, no movement. And to make matters worse, we were stuck within twenty-feet of the dreaded Check Point Jones.

"Cyclone 4-6, this is Cyclone-5, over," I radioed.

No reply from Bennick.

"Cyclone 4-6, this is Cyclone-5, over."

Again, no reply.

"Cyclone 4-6, this is Cyclone-5, over."

No reply.

The disabled ASV lost complete power, and lost power in the most dangerous places in Iraq, most dangerous according to me…Check Point Jones, and to make matters worse, it was just after midnight.

"Can you believe this?" I mumbled to my driver. "Can you actually believe this? Of all places to break down at night, just meters from Jones…can you stinking believe this at all?"

My driver sat in total silence. He had witnessed the hasty attacks while navigating on the feared Jones's roundabout. The rockets flung toward our Hummers as we strolled by. This was a spot in Iraq that was feared and detested, but again we dared not to travel on. We were too brave or maybe too stupid. Whatever the case, we drove it, convoyed it, and fought it. Jones was Jones. We *had* to patrol this dangerous traffic circle and slumped in our Hummer's seats each time we passed by, expecting the best and safest result but prepared for the worse, a fiery death by the evil hands of the insurgency that had plagued the area.

I quickly collected myself and called the lead pair of vehicles of our convoy to stop and return to the disabled ASV, and I continued to mumble to my truck crew that I did not like this situation at all as we sat in total darkness. With the destruction we inflicted at the White Apartments and sense of victory we had recently savored, I loathed having our convoy stalled at Check Point Jones, feeling alone and vulnerable in total darkness. I had horrifying experiences at Check Point Jones and did not want to spend one extra second near this dangerous roundabout.

My gun truck driver knew to back up and away from the troubled ASV, providing a safe distance and space between the two vehicles stuck in danger's way. I radioed to Sergeant Hobson at the operations shack of our situation, and that we would tow the downed ASV back to Camp Ramadi with our sole remaining and operational ASV. The ASV was so heavy; it would take another ASV or larger to tow back to Camp Ramadi. That was the only option available. It would take valuable time to hook and tow the incapacitated ASV, but that was what we had to do and do on that dark, moonless night.

TB was in the disabled ASV and could not hear the radio traffic. In the darkness, our lead gun truck turned around and came back to Check Point Jones to find our troubled ASV dead in the road. But as the operational ASV backed to hook cables to the downed machine for the tow back to Camp Ramadi, the recovery attempt turned worse. TB sent a message to me that I'll never forget as we were conducting rear security at the feared Check Point Jones.

"Cyclone-5, this is Cyclone-4-6, over," TB said in his usual calm tenure.

"Five."

"Total loss of power in my second ASV."

I listened with a feeling of complete helplessness. Two disabled ASVs with nothing to recover them with.

A long pause followed that seemed a lifetime, and I sat motionless in my gun truck.

"Cyclone-1, this is Cyclone-5, over."

"Go," a reluctant Sergeant Hobson replied.

"Requesting recovery team at Check Point Jones as soon as possible, Five out."

I hated everything about Check Point Jones. I did not like the position my truck and our convoy was stuck and stalled within inches of Check Point Jones, and I wanted out of there. A quick check of the pair of ASV trucks appeared dreadful. We were a four-vehicle convoy trapped just east of Check Point Jones and simply sitting ducks for the enemy to destroy with ease. I continued to check all areas of threat near Jones as 152nd soldiers continued to troubleshoot the downed ASVs and the recovery effort. The Hummers could not in any way pull the heavy loaded-down ASVs back to Camp Ramadi although we were just a few hundred meters from the safety of Ogden Gate.

Sergeant First Class Laddy, as many of the 152nd soldiers were, stayed posted in the operations shack that night, listening to our desperate call for help from Check Point Jones. Laddy knew exactly where we were. He was familiar with the area and knew just where Check Point Jones was, and that it was a very dangerous location. Marc had been on many convoys throughout Ramadi to check on his junior mechanics assigned to police stations and to assist with recovery missions. He knew the roads very well.

Sergeant First Class Laddy quickly assembled a team to rush to our troubled location for recovery without hesitation or fear of personal harm. That was his style. The senior mechanic was the best in theater in my mind. We convoyed together with critical supplies and personnel from Indianapolis to New Orleans in support of hurricane relief efforts just a year earlier with great success. I was credited with the Meritorious Service Medal from the Thirty-Eighth Infantry Division commander for our multiple accomplishments during the disaster mission, but the praise should have gone to all of us. The medal, known as the MSM, I did not want, specifically in front of the guys who made the mission successful, but I had to, and I reluctantly accepted.

As Sergeant First Class Laddy's recovery team arrived, a squad of Bradley's leaving the White Apartments pulled to our near right side of the troubled convoy. The Bradley's senior-ranking soldier popped his head out of a hatch and yelled, "You okay?"

I, to this day, do not know who he was or what his rank was, but that did not matter that night. The First Armored soldier did not know who I was or even asked.

"We need a pair of ASVs pulled back to camp!" I begged.

Without hesitation, a pair of Bradleys whipped in front of the disabled ASVs and hooked both up within seconds for the tow back to Camp Ramadi. As Sergeant Laddy's recovery convoy pulled up and straddled our convoy, he noticed the hasty recovery from the Bradley Fighting Vehicles and immediately had his team circle the distressed convoy for much needed additional security.

Sergeant First Class Laddy served during the Persian Gulf War and was assigned to the Twenty-Fourth Infantry Division. He was very familiar with armored vehicles and their nature. Marc was perfect and was always able to adapt to any situation at hand.

I could hear Laddy's radio transmissions from the distance but paid little attention to his commands. I knew his leadership and common sense were always reliable, and I never second-guessed him. I focused on the ASVs being hooked up to the Bradley's and getting back to Camp Ramadi safely and without anyone getting hurt.

The flawless recovery was greatly appreciated by the convoy I was returning to camp with. Check Point Jones was not only a horrible spot to drive through but a worse spot to be stuck at, feeling hopeless and susceptible.

As the Bradleys dragged our downed pair of ASVs through the checkpoint and banked north on Route Jones, it was a great feeling to see Ogden Gate's entryway ahead. Returning to Ogden was a blessing and a welcoming sight. We limped in the gate and cleared all weapons, drawing a giant sigh of relief. It was a short trip up the road to our 152nd motor pool, and the Bradley crews came to a halt near signal hill. I waved to the Bradley crews after they unhooked our broken machines. They returned the wave and headed north to brigade. There was no rank, no saluting, no awards…just soldiers taking care of soldiers in the need of help. We would have done the same for the Bradley squad, and we were grateful.

As I checked in with Sergeant Hobson to give a 100 percent accountability and equipment report as "mission completed," a radio transmission streamed in from third platoon that was returning from the White Apartments.

"Cyclone-5, this is Cyclone-3-6. Requesting you pick up and deliver twenty-four hot meals from the mess hall to my platoon, over," demanded Starnes.

I then realized that the dining facility was to close in ten minutes, and I did not reply.

Starnes must have been at the White Apartments and was told to return to Camp Ramadi following my return. He could possibly miss the dining hall closing and expected me to fetch his platoon's dinners that evening.

COSTS OF WAR

The cost of victory did not come easy in the Anbar Province during the surge. "Old Ironsides" saw eighty-five soldiers, sailors, and marines killed in action during the Anbar Awakening with over five hundred wounded during nine tough months of getting to this point of victory. American Enterprise Institute's Frederick Kagan praised MacFarland and labelled the Al Anbar Province fight, "the Gettysburg of this (Iraq) War." Kagen, a former professor of military history at the US Military Academy at West Point, influenced the strategic thinking of the secretary of defense Robert Gates with the essay, "We're Not the Soviets in Afghanistan," that influenced the increases of troops in the Iraq for the surge.

One of the marines who was killed during MacFarland's command was Maj. Megan Malia Leilani McClung, born in Hawaii and called the islands her home. While serving as a public affairs officer in the Anbar Province, Major McClung was killed on December 6, 2006, just outside of Camp Ramadi. On that chilly, December morning, Major McClung was escorting fellow Marine and Fox News's retired, Lt. Col. Oliver North in and around the Ramadi area along with several Newsweek journalists. The Humvee McClung was in rolled over a massive IED that completely destroyed McClung's gun truck. The blast instantly killed McClung along with Army Capt. Travis Patriquin and Army Spec. Vincent Pomante.

The major was a naval academy graduate and always had a smile. She was very friendly to everyone she met and had just a few weeks remaining in Iraq, finishing up a one-year deployment with the Marine Corps Reserves. The crew was travelling to visit Sattar, but the driver of the vehicle in which McClung was a passenger was inexperienced and worked primarily on night shift for the brigade. The lead vehicle of the convoy swerved left of a strange metal object in the road, just two hundred meters from a tower that was manned by Iraqis. All remaining vehicles in the convoy swerved except for the vehicle that the major was a passenger in. Inexperience and perhaps exhaustion was ruled the reason the junior enlisted driver failed to follow the path of the lead vehicles.

An enemy pressure plate explosive was said to have been placed within twelve hours of the fatal explosion.

We were furious of the news after hearing of the Hummer's blast, specifically that the blast was within sight of a coalition guard tower that was manned by Iraqis. An investigation was ordered, but an investigation could not bring the truck's crew of three back to us.

Captain Patriquin was someone special to Colonel MacFarland and the Ready First team. The multitalented captain was best known for his huge smile but better known for his PowerPoint presentations in what he called "Iraq for Dummies" that included simple graphs and humorous stick figures. Captain Patriquin's laid-back personality and casual style of leadership made planning simple for all to understand. Patriquin spoke five languages and was fluent in the Arabic language. He always sported a thick Iraqi-style moustache, and his guidance was vital during the recruiting of local Iraqis in joining the "Anbar Awakening." Iraqi leadership bestowed Captain Patriquin the name *wissam*. In English, it means "warrior." The army captain's foresight and ability to reach out to the locals fine-tuned cooperation and effort in the fight for Anbar.

McClung was the first female United States Marine Corps officer killed in combat during the Iraq War and was buried at Arlington National Cemetery, Section 60, surrounded by hundreds of other Iraqi veterans that were also killed in action while serving in Iraq.

XO TO TQ

A few weeks after the pair of battles at the White Apartments, I was moved to TQ north. The small northern section of the TQ air base covered an area approximately six or seven square miles. This area of Al Anbar was generally quiet regarding threats or attacks on coalition forces. A Marine Corps colonel was commanding the north side of TQ, and a dining facility was recently added to the northern compound along with a small post office and firing range.

I found it strange being so close to Fallujah that TQ was considered a safe area. The main base was built by the British after World War I and Route Michigan ran through the massive air base. Habbaniyah was a small quiet town just west of TQ that was abundant with farms, and the town had a few small factories. TQ north had a small airstrip with a dozen or so drones that would be dispatched for intelligence gathering, and our living quarters and operations cell were located on the far east area of the compound. The Euphrates River was to our north, and a large mountain range was to our far south. TQ's main side was also ran primarily by the Marine Corps and had a large shopping area. We liked being on the quiet northern side of the base. TQ main was flat and very dusty with cargo aircraft and helicopters flying in and out all day and all night.

Just west of TQ was a fairly small Iraqi military base located on the north side of Route Michigan. A thirty-man team of men from the

144

Philippines was recently contracted to bring the compound up to livable standards. A large water tank was installed, roads were upgraded, two watchtowers were erected, walls were plastered and painted, and a soccer field was added in the middle of the camp. The camp also had a small jail, capable to house up to thirty or thirty-five inmates. We were to assist the Iraqi police there and help out with their mission of policing the roads and neighborhoods. The IPs at Habbaniyah were very proud to be policemen. These IPs were very educated and proud of their families and town. They arrogantly enjoyed wearing the dark-blue uniform and shoulder brassard made of leather with bright white IP capital letters identifying them as active Iraqi police.

Our mission with the IPs that were just west of TQ was simple, and that was to make them successful. Uniforms, training, recruiting, ammunition, weapons, and the main issue at hand was payday. Payday was the first day of every calendar month, and we were *not* to miss that day.

The IPs near TQ were great to work with. Several spoke perfect English, and a few knew English fairly well. I had my own interpreter, so communication was not an issue at all. Many of our 152nd soldiers at TQ were catching on to the Iraqi language and were able to have lengthy conversations with the local people with ease. The police chief, who wore the rank of lieutenant colonel, was a very calm man and in his late forties, and he had five young children ranging from two to twelve years old. The chief lived on the compound with his family, and we took that as a positive due to he felt safe to house his family inside the station's fencing. Family was very important to the Iraqis, specifically in Habbaniyah.

We also had six IPLOs that lived and operated out of TQ north that were to assist our 152nd team with the local IPs. I met each one shortly after my arrival to TQ north but was not very impressed with this crew of civilians. The TQ IPLOs were not as eager to convoy to police stations as the Ramadi team. IPLOs at this base admitted that they were once police officers back in the states but were under investigation or fired from their previous positions as officers back home. I was concerned.

While at our new IP station, I worked closely with Iraqi police-man Lt. Kaden Wathic. He was assigned to the motor pool and also led a small checkpoint near the station on Michigan. Lieutenant Wathic spoke perfect English and was very, very proud of his uniform and his duty as an Iraqi policemen who protected the town of his family and friends. We instantly became friends and were rarely apart, allowing my senior enlisted noncommissioned officer, Sgt. 1st Cl. David VanKamp, to use our assigned translator, Romeo. Romeo was from Tekrit, a large town in northern Iraq. Romeo spoke English very well and did a great job translating, but his greatest strength was his friendship and loyalty to our team.

Iraqi sergeant Samir Amar was the police station's top mechanic and was always with Lieutenant Wathic. Sergeant Amar could fix anything. He was very loyal and jumped to his boss's every command.

Our team really fit in well with the IPs at Habbaniyah.

Sergeant VanKamp was a man of few words but held the platoon together very well. He was an avid fisherman and worked at Delta Faucet in Indianapolis while not deployed. We roomed together at TQ and got along very well. I knew he could run operations on his own, but higher headquarters wanted me at TQ to help expand the mission to clear Route Michigan and choke out the insurgency's gateway to Baghdad.

The only thing that bothered me about the senior NCO were his odd pajama shorts that he wore nightly following patrols and long days spent at police stations. The shorts were dark blue with cartoons of yellow rubber duckies. I meant to ask the six-foot senior NCO why this specific choice of underwear, but I never did, I just tried to ignore them. Maybe VanKamp's wife bought the strange rubber duckie undies for him for his birthday, or wrapped them as a Christmas gift, but the gentle giant was afraid to explain to his wife that he didn't like them.

We were able to freely convoy east toward Fallujah from TQ on Route Michigan, but coalition forces were forbidden to take the route west from TQ to Ramadi. And this was a problem we desperately needed to fix. There were two available routes to get back and forth from TQ to Ramadi, Route Mobile to the north, or several alternate routes from the south. The northern route, Route Mobile, was a main corridor from Ramadi to Baghdad. Mobile was a major highway that resembled many American freeways that had wide medians, two lanes each way. There were many overpasses along the way, and Mobile had wide shoulders on each side of the well-paved highway that was a luxury compared to most roads in Iraq. Route Mobile was responsible for many, many roadside bombs, booby traps, and sniper fire. Several canals that were fed by the Euphrates skirted the highway, making easy enemy hiding spots and ways to travel by small boats at night without being detected. The tall grass that grew wild on the sides of the waterways were perfect to duck into. It was nearly impossible to fish out a suspected insurgent or find hidden weapon stashes. The southern alternate routes were very dangerous to travel on as well. The southern roads did not have shoulders, no medians, and were one-lane roads with sand mounds and small hills that could easily hide snipers or an enemy ambush. Which was safer? It was dangerous either way, Route Mobile to the north or the alternate routes that ran to the south.

The territory between TQ and Camp Ramadi was basically a quiet stretch of highway that consisted of small towns and plenty of farming communities. Route Michigan between TQ and Ramadi was a well-paved two-lane road but considered an alternate coalition route but a vital passage and direct line of passage from TQ to Camp Ramadi. Higher desperately wanted this alternate route in our hands and for our use. With the enemy threat diminishing in Ramadi and insurgent supplies and equipment now choked of easy travel through Ramadi, this was the perfect time to change Michigan from *red* to *green*. Travel time from TQ to Ramadi on Michigan was a fraction compared to the northern or southern routes. Less time on the roads meant less opportunity of enemy attacks. Securing Route Michigan from TQ to Ramadi would mean additional territory gained for our effort and add to the overall freedom of movement for coalition forces.

Small towns that were scattered along Route Michigan between TQ and Ramadi were known to be the wealthier areas to live in. One town, just six or seven miles west of TQ, was Husaybah. The town of Husaybah was located on the north side of Route Michigan and had beautiful homes, perfectly paved roads, many business owners lived in Husaybah, and tribal leadership owned huge beautiful mansions. I was told this area of Anbar was ruled by the Khalidiya tribe who were very wealthy and powerful in the Arabic world. Some of the Husaybah homes were three-stories tall made with two-foot thick cement walls, and most had huge entryways and stunning foyers. Many homes in Husaybah had small gardens nearby, and life was quiet and prosperous in this quiet area of Iraq. But the people did not want anything to do with coalition forces or anything to do with the insurgency as well. These people wanted to be left alone and could take care of their own families without any help from anyone. The town had several soccer fields, plenty of schools, and littered with shopping districts. Husaybah was a discreet town, and the people seemed generally reclusive, but children were everywhere, and they loved to play soccer. Our convoys rarely caught the attention of kids playing soccer along Route Michigan. Most ignored the endless traffic of helicopters that flew in and out of the busy nearby TQ airfield. They just wanted to be left alone.

Husaybah was a primary location for a police station. A police station set up at Husaybah was critical due to it was at the halfway point between Fallujah and Ramadi. An additional IP station to the west of TQ was ideal and very critical according to our higher leadership, and I strongly agreed. We lived fairly close to Husaybah. It only took four or five minutes to get there from TQ. I gladly volunteered to set up and work out of the future Husaybah Police Station, and I knew we could completely control Route Michigan at this location within a few months, maybe a few weeks.

During a recent briefing, the marine leadership at TQ looked at me and VanKamp as if we were crazy for saying we could clear Michigan in a short amount of time, but they allowed us to work

Husaybah without interruption or involvement. We were on our own with the IPs.

One sunny morning, our platoon-size convoy rambled west on Route Michigan to meet up with leaders of Husaybah's soon-to-be police station. We pulled in with four heavily armored Hummers that were locked and loaded with machine guns mounted on each gun truck. We were loaded with high-powered radios that could easily reach TQ, and we also had our much-needed jamming devises made to block IED triggers. While pulling into the parking lot of the future police station that morning, I noticed long stretches of barbed wire and armed sentries protecting a small driveway that led to a three-story white house that resembled a small castle. Soon, a pair of well-dressed men exited from tall wooden doors of the home, eager to meet the visiting Americans. We were warmly welcomed inside the magnificent home, amazed by the home's marble floors and a spiral staircase.

The view impressed all that entered this small palace, complete with a ten-foot wide chandelier in the massive foyer. The palace was on loan from a tribal chief who gave the okay for his Husaybah home to be used as an Iraqi police station. But the formal title of "police station" had not yet been awarded to the leadership of this lavish house. That title of being declared a formal police station had to be earned. The station needed policemen, and well-disciplined and trained policemen. TQ had a police academy located on the far north side of the base that was built on the southern banks of the Euphrates River. The academy could train up to 250 cadets at a time that would later be scattered throughout the region following graduation. Training usually took two to three months, followed by formal ceremonies with plenty of Iraqi and American high-ranking visitors to dazzle the beaming IP graduates.

The pair of Iraqi men that shepherded me, Sergeant VanKamp, Romeo, and a pair of infantrymen into the grand home that seemed to gleam in the early morning Iraqi sunshine were very eager to have their loaned home become a formal police station. The humble and hospitable Iraqis stressed that the future station desperately needed to get policemen trained up, then dispatched on the Husaybah roads as soon as possible.

The leaders of the Husaybah soon-to-be police station, in my opinion, were very educated, driven, but a bit cautious of any visitors. While speaking with the men with the help from Romeo's translation, an Iraqi man was sitting perfectly still in the corner of what was known as the station chief's main office of the miraculous home. The office was once a bedroom, it appeared, but now the room was filled with a few desks, bookcases with several laptop computers. The walls were decorated with a few maps taped to the plaster walls. We chatted, drank tea, and spoke about Husaybah for several hours and how IPs could provide safety and security for the town. There was very little crime or trouble in the area, and the well-dressed Iraqis wanted to keep it that way.

I later found that the quiet man in the corner could speak perfect English. He was secretly listening to our sidebar conversations that Romeo did not pass on just to read us a little better and let the leadership know what we were saying during side conversations. I did not blame them for this approach. We did not know them, they did not know us, but we were brought in as instant friends and treated like family. The warm welcome was very appreciated.

One of the first tasks at hand for Husaybah was establishing a key checkpoint on Route Michigan, and we wanted this checkpoint near the main gate of the fortified palace. On the south side of the massive home had twenty-five to thirty bullet holes that appeared to have been fired from Route Michigan. The bullet holes were a grim reminder that the area was not in any way 100 percent safe or secure, and we had to remain on our toes although we felt warmly welcomed in Husaybah.

Within a few days, the Husaybah checkpoint was set up and was an instant hit. Concrete walls were delivered to the checkpoint and set in place by forklifts, and a few dozen sheets of plywood created a roof, and a few cammo nets were hung over walls to keep the dust from creeping in the dining area and sleeping quarters. Four or five men staffed the newly erected checkpoint, and Route Michigan was to be monitored twenty-four hours a day, every day of the week without exception. A generator provided lighting at night, and a few water tanks were installed. A flagpole was brought to the checkpoint, and the Iraq flag proudly waived atop of the checkpoint's sleeping area.

We delivered a few additional concrete barriers with 150 sandbags that were stacked ten-feet high near walkways for protection. Security personnel were trained to check each vehicle, ensuring there were no illegal weapons or ammunition passing through the area. Pamphlets were brought to the checkpoint that had images of high-profile terrorists moving through the area. Spotting a high-profile insurgent was critical, and orders were to swiftly capture any enemy VIP at any cost. Future police recruits conducted foot patrols in the city of Husaybah. The IPs were very proud to patrol their own city streets, and the people truly wanted safe streets and towns just as badly as we Americans did.

The station was equipped with several brand-new white four-door Ford F-350 trucks with the words *Iraqi Police* neatly painted on all doors. Each truck was fitted with sirens, a bullhorn, and a machine gun mounted in the back of each truck bed. The trucks were very impressive yet intimidating. I do not know how the expensive IP trucks were paid for, but they were there, and we could not have been successful without them and the crews who were manning each truck.

We felt safe, and rumor was a group of Americans dressed in suits, delivered suitcases of cash to the local tribal leadership along the critical route that ran through Husaybah. Cash speaks in the Middle East, and with the loads of donated cash, we became "instant friends" with the people in Husaybah. This cash tactic was also heavily used in Afghanistan. These people in suits must have been from the State Department, but they would arrive in an area with millions of American dollars to hire local soldiers or IPs. Equipment and trainers soon followed. Overall, pay them and fight with them or later fight against them. We didn't care what had happened. We were friends and now patrolling with them.

An additional checkpoint was added a few miles west of the Husaybah police station to beef up security on Route Michigan. Seven hundred sandbags were delivered along with a gun tower and a small generator to light up the roadway and surrounding farmlands at night. Twenty IPs manned this checkpoint night and day, and threat levels dropped dramatically. After a week, attacks dropped to zero between Ramadi and Fallujah.

Route Michigan between TQ and Ramadi was soon considered *secure* with the newly erected and manned checkpoints. This was an amazing accomplishment. With the success, Husaybah was then declared an official station, and the policemen were formally honored the title of Iraq policemen. With Route Michigan clear and safe for travel within a very short amount of time, additional funding and vehicles arrived at the station a few days after the dedication ceremony. Michigan was now *green* and completely safe for coalition travel.

The marines at TQ were stunned that Michigan was now green and in coalition control.

Surprisingly, Sergeant Amar was not at the Husaybah Police Station's dedication ceremony. I was sure he would be there for the celebration. We then realized Amar had not been to work for over one week, and he was about to be fired as an Iraqi policeman.

Lieutenant Wathic approached Sergeant VanKamp and begged us not to fire the mechanic due to his five-year-old daughter was dying. She had been very ill for ten days, and Amar's family was expecting her to die soon. Sergeant Amar adored his daughter and always spoke of her with great admiration. She was the apple of his eye, and he treasured her.

"Why didn't you tell us?" I asked Wathic.

"His daughter only wants to eat candy," Wathic added with pain in his voice. "She will not live long and is losing weight. She will not eat nourishing foods, just candy."

We knew Sergeant Amar adored his young daughter, but we were not aware she was deathly ill. We returned to base that evening to scrounge up any and every medicine we could get our hands on from aspirin to Tylenol. We gathered fresh water, power bars, stashed fresh fruit from the dining hall in our cargo pockets, found a few toys, and gathered a bag filled with every flavor of Gatorade drink we could collect for the girl.

Handing the gifts to Lieutenant Wathic the next morning, we asked to relay a message to Sergeant Amar, "Stay at home with your family." Three days later, Sergeant Amar returned to work, and his daughter was as fine as could be. We were thrilled of the news and collected $57 American dollars for Sergeant Amar to help with any needed medical costs for his cherished daughter.

Our team never had the chance to meet the girl, but we were sure Sergeant Amar and his family were grateful for the gifts. Did we save her life? I don't know. But in my mind, I hope we did.

Husaybah's police chief could not be happier with his station being formally declared an Iraqi Police Station. The chief grabbed me one early morning and would not let me go. The chief's smile was never larger, and he seemed larger than life itself.

"We are a station!" the chief yelled. "We are official!"

RED ROOM

Fallujah was Marine Territory. The US Marines were in charge of Fallujah and territory west of Fallujah, so basically I worked for the Marine Corps while at TQ north. The corps' territory also covered the massive TQ airbase, and the many small farming towns surrounding the area including Habbaniyah and Husaybah. Basically, the Marines owned the eastern side of Al Anbar Province that covered roughly 100 square miles.

Marines were okay to work with, but the local SEAL team was fantastic to work with while I was at TQ north. This elite team owned a small one-story building near us on TQ north that they slept and operated out of. When the SEAL team was not on mission and back on TQ north, they were usually hanging out in front of their secluded building, enjoying the morning's warm sunshine and simply chatting with each other as if they were hanging out back in the states having a cup of coffee on a street corner. They were so relaxed that visitors or guests would never guess that these guys were actual SEALs, the tip-top of all American special operations forces. They did not wear rank, not even name tags. They were just simply there in desert camouflage and designer sunglasses. They wanted to keep a very, very low-profile. These guys would not even brag about being in the SEALs, they were just there with us in the battle.

The 152 guys at TQ north knew this fact of the SEALs, and respected their privacy and time-honored traits and low-profile manors.

Marines at TQ thought themselves as better than any branch of the United States military, and really didn't want to associate with us Army guys, specifically national guard soldiers that were desperately thrown into the fray in Iraq. But the SEALs could see the advantage of operating with each of the services, and heavily relied on our IP team to add to their effort in Iraq. We and the IPs were a combat multiplier for the SEALs, and SEALs use every and any advantage to deliver success on the battlefield. And the 152 infantry guys were a perfect bunch to add to their war chest.

I took this as a privilege to be with the SEALs and an honor to work with them.

Our 152 team was usually tasked as the TQ SEAL quick response force—better known as QRF—and at times assisted in low-profile operations with the Navy's elite. And the SEALs knew our team had just under two hundred Iraqi Policemen that were always eager to answer the call in the eastern province of Anbar.

I later realized why the SEALs reached out to our Army National Guard unit in place of the Marine security team assigned to TQ north. I witnessed the Marines comically attempt to mount a 50-caliber machine gun on a gun truck, the Marines simply struggled that day. Several of our 152 guys strolled over to visit the troubled Marines to help them out that morning.

With hundreds of missions ran throughout the country during our stay, 152 guys could mount a gun on a gun truck's turret within a few seconds. The SEALs noticed and we had greatly impressed them with our skills. We were the go-to guys for the SEALs and I humbly appreciated this informal honor.

Our senior Marine in the eastern Anbar Police sector, Lt. Colonel Robert Gout, was promoted to colonel soon after I had arrived at TQ north. This was a well-deserved promotion in my mind as well as VanKamp's. Following Gout's promotion and transfer to serve as the Anbar Provence chief of Iraqi Police operations at nearby Camp Blue

Diamond, we were left to answer to Gout's deputy at TQ north that specialized in the military police field, Marine Captain James Downs.

Downs was a very book-smart and brilliant Marine officer that put his heart and soul into the IP mission in Eastern Anbar. He led this sector of Anbar with ease, an area that was slotted a Lt. Colonel position, for just under a month until word was out that Gout's replacement was now inbound from the states following a few weeks of training at Quantico. We at TQ north knew it was just a matter of time until a new Lt. Colonel would arrive to take over for the recently promoted Gout, and he was now just a few short days away from being *"in-country"*. The new field grade officer reported to TQ north very late on a hot June Iraqi night, and Downs humbly and respectfully returned as the loyal and trusting deputy chief as soon as the Lt. Colonel had landed at TQ. Just as any good Marine would.

It took several days for some reason, but our 152 guys eventually met the recently arrived Marine Lt. Colonel Richard Gire, now tasked to lead the North TQ IP teams and eastern Anbar. Gire had been retired from the Marine Corps for well over a decade, and volunteered to return to active duty service and serve in Iraq or Afghanistan. Either war was fine with him, he didn't care. Gire just wanted a taste of combat, this was something he had never experienced during his 20 years with the Marines prior to retiring in 1996. But Gire wanted combat experience, and this is what he was delivered…lead the IPs in troubled eastern Anbar.

Gire stood at 5-feet and maybe 5 inches tall, and tipped the scale at 135 pounds at most. Gire was just over 50-years old, with jet-white hair. Gire reminded me of former presidential candidate H. Ross Perot, and he chose to carry a large 12-gage military-issued shot gun in place of the typical Berretta pistol, a weapon standard for an American field grade officer on the battlefield. The shotgun was just about as tall as the chief was, and Gire always sported the weapon to his front, barrel pointed to the ground, sling strapped across his back.

I was later told that the base armorer issued Gire the shotgun but his supply room wasn't authorized to stock the weapon's specific ammunition. The supply sergeant insisted Gire accept the Berretta pistol but the chief refused, demanding the oversized, shiny shotgun regardless of having ammunition to arm the weapon with. The shotgun sparkled in the bright Iraqi sun and was very intimidating, yet useless if needed on the battlefield. Useless unless you wanted to smack an insurgent over the head with the buttstock, or prop it on a pair of footlockers and have a congo line in the TQ north courtyard. A weapon without ammo was awfully strange according to me as well as VanKamp. We both stuck with our M4 rifle and Berretta secured to our right thigh as a backup.

For the first few weeks at TQ north, Gire kept his distance from our team and the other units that supported the Iraq Police effort in the area. As our 152 team was finishing a convoy brief prior to leaving the north-side compound of TQ, Gire appeared out of nowhere, and said quietly "every day, and every mission you men leave this compound for...I say a prayer for each one of you." We thanked the chief and threw a few salutes his way, then returned to our briefing as Gire quietly strolled off. Not sure where he was going, but he disappeared between a few buildings and we finished up our brief and left the compound.

The Chief's words seemed a bit strange, but we warmly welcomed the modest blessings. VanKamp usually held an emotionless stare at Gire, not saying much or even acknowledging the field grade Marine's presence.

Gire approached me early one evening in our secure email room that was recently named the "*Red Room*" due to a fresh coat of red paint on the entrance door. The door also had the words "classified area" in bright yellow. To enter the room, or to have a secure email with authorization to the classified web, a secret-level clearance was needed and approved only by the Department of Defense. The process was not too difficult to complete, but a background check was required for access.

The Red Room was a neat place to be. The Red Room was a quiet, secluded area that was the size of a typical American bedroom, cooled by a small air conditioner in the far-side corner, and a safe-place to gather intel for the next day's mission—thanks to our treasured intelligence community.

I cannot thank our intel community enough for their tireless work, work that I can guarantee saved many, many lives for us in Iraq during the surge.

The chief looked over at me from his terminal and asked, "What is the main concern with your guys at the stations?"

"Well, right now," I answered. "the Insurgency is recruiting in Husaybah."

"Recruiting?" Gire asked with a puzzled look.

"The IPs have found flyers around their town that have been delivered at night," I replied. "They are offering better pay than what the Iraqi Ministry of Defense is offering…they are actively recruiting in the area."

Gire sat quietly.

"The Insurgency is also recruiting for women to approach coalition with suicide vests" I added. "The bomber's family will be paid for the attack once completed…so we are being very cautious of local women—or men possibly dressed as women—approaching our trucks or checkpoints."

After a slight pause the chief stood up and left the Red Room without saying a word, which was not the usual for Gire.

The newly painted door to the Red Room quickly shut, and I took a few moments to question what the abrupt departure was all about.

But I returned to my research. The Iraqi Police payday was in the morning and I was gathering any intel regarding the Insurgency's recent recruiting and recent threats against police and coalition near payday. The threats had me very concerned, yet not in fear of the next day's mission.

We were completing our tenth IP payday in Iraq. Payday was something Sergeant VanKamp kept close tabs on. Every payday we had completed, meant that we were one month closer to completing our twelve-month combat mission in Iraq and a little bit closer returning to our home state of Indiana, the *Hoosier State*. We were expecting only two remaining paydays left in county, sixty days and some change. This kept our spirits up, and hopes high. We were ready to go *home*.

VanKamp and I were the only 152 Cyclone Soldiers at TQ north that were married. The others on our team were young, lucky to have a girlfriend back in the states waiting on them to return home following their year of combat in Iraq. We were the oddballs at TQ north… to be married. The others just seemed so young without many cares or worries.

As our convoy pulled up to the Habbaniyah Police station for payday morning, the sun was just beginning to break over the quiet, farming province. The historic Euphrates River, that ran to the station's north perimeter, glistened in the early morning's sunrise and people of the city began to kick-off their usual day that began with large speakers delivering the morning's sacred Islamic prayers. The morning prayers were loud enough to cover the entire city and echoed far enough that most farms and factories that skirted the city could easily hear the morning's entreaty.

A squad of IPs greeted our team as we were pulling up to the main entrance of the Habbaniyah Police Station. The huge iron gates quickly opened, and we were waved into the compound with wide smiles along with warm Iraqi greetings *"salaam alaikum"*. It was payday, and the police always rolled out the red carpet for Americans delivering payday cash. VanKamp had payday operations handled with true perfection. Night shift IPs were paid first, and checkpoint IPs were second. Police that were off duty followed and on-duty police were the final to be paid. We would start paying the IPs sharply at 7 in the morning, and we could easily be finished by 8:30. Completed prior to the day's temperatures reaching over 80 degrees, allowing IP patrols to roll out of the station to proudly serve the area's residents.

We had a perfect IP payday planned, we had thought.

As our convoy pulled in front of the police station's headquarters, we noticed four additional hummers arriving at the station's main gate.

"Marines are here," VanKamp mentioned.

I noticed the convoy of Marine gun trucks clear the gate, and then enter into the compound's staging area, near the station's headquarters building.

Gire stepped out of the lead hummer and directly marched toward me with two of his security detail.

"What is going on?" I asked VanKamp, as he silently looked on with a blank gaze.

"We are taking over payday operations," the chief instructed as his detail intercepted the boxes of cash and entered the station's headquarters.

"Please, excuse me sir?" I asked Gire.

"We are taking over payday operations." Gire repeated. "I was told you are not doing a good job with the IPs so we will take over, and we will take over now."

At this point, 180 IPs were standing in line that stretched over 50 yards long, eagerly awaiting the monthly paycheck of 3,500 Dinar—equivalent to $110 American Dollars.

Gire then turned to his interpreter and stated, "Tell all of the police to go in the courtyard!"

The interpreter followed the chief's command and barked in Arabic the instructions.

IPs quickly scurried to the station's courtyard just south of the station's headquarters building. A large dust cloud followed the stampede of policemen excited to hear what the American, dawning the large shotgun across his chest, had to say. Gire strolled over the edge of the courtyard, overlooking the modest IPs, with his oversized 12-gage shotgun strung across his body, with his interpreter stationed to his left. The chief then spent ten minutes introducing himself to the crowd of policemen, policemen that were patiently listening to the American explaining that he was their new boss, as the IPs closely kept their eyes on the main doors of the headquarters that held their treasured monthly earnings.

VanKamp and I quietly wandered away from the headquarters building and cooled off under the shade of a few trees near the major's office to observe the impromptu briefing by the chief. Gire kept talking and talking...and the IPs sat motionless in the courtyard.

Temperatures were quickly heating up as the sun rose over the compound, beating on the backs of the IPs as the chief continued to speak, his interpreter echoing each sentence. Much like the IPs, I quickly became lost in the moment as the chief rambled on.

VanKamp ordered our 152 guys back to our staged gun trucks to relax. The Marines had taken over, and we were not to assist today with payday operations. We were pushed to the side and left as bystanders.

"What is this all about, sir?" VanKamp asked.

"I don't know..." I answered, as the chief's briefing went into 20 minutes.

VanKamp and I then made our way to the front gate, and stood in the shade of the station's tallest gun tower. Gire continued his speech as IPs began to fidget and become impatient. Today was payday, not lecture day for the IPs.

My mind began to drift as the chief continued to chatter, but my attention was redirected when I heard the chief speak about the Insurgency's recruiting flyers that had been scattered around this portion of the Anbar Province.

"And if any of you quit, and join the Insurgency," the chief stated. "We will find you...and we will kill you."

I was shocked. VanKamp stood in silence.

"Now get in line for pay!" the chief ordered.

Chaos then erupted. The herd of 180 policemen dashed to the front door of the headquarters building, wanting to be the first to get paid as VanKamp and myself witnessed the disaster from afar.

Gire began barking orders, orders in English that the IPs could not understand. The Chief's interpreter became lost in the mess, and the station's deputy and major could only watch in horror.

Several fights between policemen erupted, and the checkpoint IPs were pushing ahead of the line to be paid and return to their post on Route Michigan. Two rounds that sounded like they were fired from a pistol zoomed over the compound.

VanKamp asked "Did those rounds come from inside the compound? Or outside of the compound?"

I wasn't sure myself, and I shrugged my shoulders.

Gire made his way to the station chief that had exited the back door of his headquarters building, not knowing what all the mess was about, and walked toward the havoc.

"This is your station!" Gire yelled to the station chief. "You fix this now!"

The station's chief, who also wore the rank of his counterpart Gire, simply turned away and returned to his office inside of the headquarters building.

Gire was left, standing at the edge of the police station's headquarters as a few policemen were being carried off for either being battered during the commotion, or victims of heat exhaustion due to being left in the sweltering heat of the Iraqi sun that July morning.

Gire slowly turned and walked to his convoy's lead vehicle that had delivered him to the police station that morning. He sadly slumped into the Hummer's passenger seat, he then took a long, deep breath as the Iraqi Policemen continued to push, shove, and elbow their way into the front door of the building that supplied their precious payday funds.

I continued to watch in disbelief as VanKamp kept his cool, as he usually did in every situation, and glimpsed into the distance. VanKamp didn't say a word.

From the courtyard marched Gire's Gunnery Sergeant, his senior non-commissioned officer at TQ north, Gunnery Sergeant Thomas "Tommy" Ashby.

The Gunnery Sergeant that I held high respect for approached me and humbly asked "How can this be fixed?"

"We can fix this…" VanKamp interrupted, with an emotionless glance. "Don't worry about it."

Being senior to both VanKamp and Ashby, I directed the conversation back to me and held a slight smile as the Gunnery Sergeant seemed completely defeated.

"Your convoy can return to TQ with the colonel," I requested. "Sergeant VanKamp can run today's operations without any problems."

Gunnery Ashby stared in silence for a few moments and knew that this was the best remedy for the situation at hand. The Marine snapped to attention, rendered a sharp salute, I then returned the salute. The Gunnery turned to the trucks while ordering his men to mount up.

A burst of dust and sand kicked up as the chief's convoy fired up and departed the IP compound's east gate, and the four trucks soon disappeared into the distance, heading eastward on Route Michigan.

VanKamp then took charge, as any great non-commissioned would, and ordered the night shift IPs to muster near the set of trees next to the headquarter's building. He then ordered the checkpoint police to stand near the shrubs that led to the jail area.

"If you do not organize," VanKamp stated with the assistance of my interpreter Romeo, "you will not be paid."

Policemen snapped to his every command as I watched from the gun tower's cooling shade. VanKamp knew each policeman by name and face. He knew just what to do.

"Line up!" VanKamp insisted. "Keep in line."

Payday continued without flaw and without incident. The IPs listened to VanKamp and respected the senior American non-commissioned officer. IPs on duty that day retuned to their posts, with huge, satisfying smiles knowing that they had earned their monthly pay. IPs not on duty that day quickly hustled home, rushing to provide for their families, buy food, pay rent. Just the fact of returning home with cash earned from serving as an "Iraqi Policemen" in their community was an honor. A well-deserved honor.

VanKamp, much as the SEALs that operated in our sector, did not expect praise or gratitude. He just wanted to work hard and lead. I recommended VanKamp for a Bronze Star Medal nearing our departure from Iraq. However, his Bronze Star was denied by our military police battalion commander. My Bronze Star was also denied by the battalion commander. "Not deserving" was the commander's strange remark for both of us.

Sadly, I had to inform VanKamp that his Bronze Star had been denied. It was very hard to do, we had cleared Route Michigan from TQ toward Ramadi. We opened police stations and checkpoints to clear Michigan that we were not even authorized to drive on, deemed "red". It was puzzling why we were denied any reward for our work. But we marched on, our team marched on. We had to and wanted to. There was no other option.

Our company's first casualty during our tour was Staff Sergeant Patrick Shannon. I had submitted a Silver Star Medal during our first few weeks at Camp Ramadi, for a selfless act under combat while severely injured. I was ordered to submit Shannon for a Bronze Star in place of the glorious honor of a Silver Star by the MPs.

Shannon was seriously injured just south of Camp Ramadi during a mortar blast that injured Several IPs, an IPLO, and himself while on a simple patrol with the Al Hurriya police. A mortar's explosion had picked up Shannon and tossed him across the street he was walking near, he was waiving to a few children peaking out of a window's curtain. The blast from the nearby mortar landing also damaged his right eye beyond repair, and left shards of metal in his legs and right arm.

Dazed and bewildered by the mortar's effects, Shannon picked himself up and carried the injured pair of IPLOs and injured policemen into an apartment complex doorway for safety as several mortars were lobbed onto the detail's position with extreme accuracy. The mortar crew was nearby, within eyeshot of the Americans and police. And the lethal rounds continued to pour on the helpless crew on patrol that December morning.

Shannon went well above and beyond that day. And I had noticed Shannon's selfless bravery, but the higher MPs did not and rejected my suggestion for the Silver Star. The medal was not downgraded, I was ordered to resubmit. My recommendation was to be the Bronze Star or nothing. I reluctantly decided on the Bronze Star, with great pain. I did not want the non-commissioned officer that had dazzled me and other leadership in the company go home without being recognized for his service in Iraq.

Maybe the battalion commander did not know or understand what we had accomplished or had done? Either Shannon or VanKamp and myself? But that does not really matter, we did a great job and had accomplished what many could not have.

THE PAYDAY MELEE

The very last IP payday at our police stations was very special to our unit. We were one step closer to going home. Sergeant VanKamp took care of all payday activities at the stations scattered throughout our sector of Anbar, and he was fantastic at coordinating the complex and busy day that was so important to the policemen and their families.

Our first stop that morning was the main Habbaniyah Station that included IPs who manned two checkpoints nearby. It was just shy of nine o'clock in the morning, and temperatures were beginning to quickly rise. But that morning, directly north of our station's main entrance, several machine gun rounds entered into the compound. One round landed between myself and VanKamp, another hit the station's power box, leaving the station without power for a few days. Spec. Jason Setton, one of our truck gunners, claimed a round bounced off his Hummer's rear hatch. Setton said he could feel the round's vibration on the back of his neck following the erratic ricochet, but he didn't flinch at all. None of us hesitated with paying the IPs, and if anything, we just ducked and went on with payday events. We had become accustomed to the dangerous everyday life in Iraq. It was just another day for us, another day in Anbar and another day in a combat zone.

IPs were not dispatched to seek out the renegade enemy snipers. Payday was far too important to the policemen. And this fact was alright with myself and VanKamp. Get the IPs paid and then we could get back to work, get back to patrolling, get back to business.

Spec. Setton later committed suicide in a movie theater in his hometown of Farmland, Indiana following our deployment. I don't know why, perhaps he had mental or emotional issues from the surge. But I do know that he was a great kid, just twenty-one years old at his death. We had several suicides following our unit's return to the states, but Jacob was closest to me during our deployment and served honorably as a soldier, an infantryman and a truck gunner.

TABLES TURNED

Each morning, prior to every mission, I would check my secure email in the Red Room for intelligence updates in our area. Day by day, I noticed threat levels decreasing, units were free to use Route Michigan between Ramadi and Fallujah, and coalition attack numbers significantly dropped in Anbar. Prior to our departure, attacks went to zero. It was a good feeling of accomplishment for our team and the Iraqis we worked with. We applied the same methods that Colonel McMaster had went by up north during Operation Restoring Rights in 2005 with his Third Armored Cav.

Romeo approached me one morning prior to a patrol with the Husaybah IPs. He also noticed the sharp decrease of violence in Al Anbar.

"We will have peace in Iraq," our interpreter stated. "One day, we will have peace."

Romeo grew up near Balad, north of Baghdad. Violence was a way of life for people in Balad. He and his family were tired of violence and war in Iraq.

Prior to our company leaving Iraq, Romeo departed TQ to go home and visit family up north and enjoy a well-earned seven-day pass. Romeo's smile beamed as he stuffed wads of American cash in hidden compartments within the soles of his boots and jumped in a taxi. The interpreter's first stop would be at his beloved parent's home in just a few hours. Romeo deserved a vacation. He had been away from family for fifteen long months interpreting for Americans in Anbar.

But bad news broke. Within an hour of Romeo's parting, his fellow translators based at our compound delivered sad news to myself and Sergeant First Class VanKamp. Romeo was captured near Baghdad and was murdered. The American cash found hidden in his boots tied the young Iraqi to working with coalition forces. He was tortured and killed by the insurgency.

We were devastated of the news and simply felt horrible for the family of Romeo whom he spoke so favorable of. We knew his parents and family were crushed beyond belief.

But Romeo reappeared later that week, and his first stop was to report to Sergeant VanKamp. His family was also told of his murder, but the news was incorrect. Romeo was alive, and the story of his killing was false. We were elated to see our top translator back at base and safe.

Romeo returned to work the next day.

Just prior to our departure early August of 2007, the new Jazeera Iraqi Police Station or JIPS opened. We could see this station from our barracks at TQ north. JIPS was located just over the Euphrates River on the north side of the historic waterway. This station was manned mostly by Abu Ali Jassim Tribal members that were primarily Habbaniyah farmers. Unlike many of our police stations, JIPS was not located in or near a town. This station was in an open field that was very remote. And when it rained, JIPS turned into the world's largest mud pie, nearly impossible to even drive near. Winds from the southwest would kick up sand, making living and working conditions a bit harsh, but the IPs seemed to like the station overall. Setting up the compound was easy compared to other police stations in metropolitan areas. The station's perimeter was over a mile away from anything. Lookout towers could easily spot distress, and convoys could quickly be dispatched to trouble without navigating through difficult city streets.

The police assigned to the Jazeera Iraqi Police Station were great fighters and soldiers. Most IPs were related to each other, and they were very tribal and faithful to each other. But a few weeks after the station's grand opening, JIPS was attacked. Sadly, the sheikh of the Abu Ali Jassim tribe was killed at the station. To make matters worse, enemy Al-Qaeda forces then hid the sheikh's body for several days, as well as the three murdered Shirtas from the Jazeera Iraqi Police Station. This was an insult to the Abu Ali Jassim tribe, as well as a violation of Islam's very strict burial rules that call for proper entombment procedures by nightfall. Everyone respected this fact of the Middle East without hesitation, but the enemy refused to honor this sacred pact, engulfing the coalition effort at JIPS stronger and as fierce as ever.

The Abu Ali Jassim tribe and other nearby tribes took this killing very personally and quickly brought the fight hard and brutal to Al-Qaeda forces in eastern Al Anbar without mercy. Insurgents of Al-Qaeda attempted to destroy a cell phone tower on the far east side of Ramadi. Locals quickly warned Abu Ali Jassim IPs, and the policemen quickly put a halt to the enemy's attempt. The threatening insurgents attempted to show their soft and kind side to the locals by warning of the explosives that were to be placed at the tower's base, but there is one thing you do not want to take away from the civilians of Anbar, cell phone signal. Iraqi Police bolted to the east side of Ramadi to rescue the tower and fight the enemy up close and personal. The fight did not last long, and the IPs destroyed the enemy quickly at the tower. This went to the core of our plan, build trust and confidence with the locals and win the war.

Our Hummers could not keep up with the IP rush to the cell tower in peril, but the IPs took care of business quickly with rapid, extreme, and deadly force. The insurgents who managed to survive the fight fled into the night never to return or threaten the policemen from JIPS that were affectionately honored with the title the "Sons of Iraq" for their fighting skills.

Cellular phones were the fastest way for locals to call for help. The insurgency thought taking out the towers would halt any calls for aid.

The recent attack on the Jazeera Iraqi Police Station also injured a small number of policemen, just burns from a nearby explosion.

Colonel MacFarland offered the station's policemen safety on Camp Blue Diamond, a small American Army site located just north of Camp Ramadi while they repaired their damaged station, but the Iraqis refused to abandon their recently damaged police station and immediately resumed patrolling. The tribesmen turned police showed their toughness, drive, and fighting spirit following the assault.

While standing up and manning police stations with supporting checkpoints along Route Michigan, large convoys were now free to roll east and west with little fear or threats of attack. Civilian car traffic tripled on Michigan that ran through the many small towns and farming villages. Soccer fields were filled with players and fans. Businesses reopened, and people quickly adjusted to the pleasant changes in the province. The one event that convinced me that Route Michigan was ours and safe, was witnessing an American soldier crossing Route Michigan near a medical station that had recently been set in place that assisted Iraqis with basic care. The soldier was on foot without a helmet. Safe enough to not need a helmet? We won.

We knew the IPs trusted our platoon following an explosion that rocked our convoy just after midnight on Route Michigan as we checked on the IP checkpoint near Husaybah. The station sent all of its men to check on us. Little did I know, Sergeant VanKamp had a training explosive to see how the convoy's newest soldiers would react if hit. Our new guys did well and did not panic following the explosion that detonated next to their Hummer behind us. The blast was so large it rattled our gun truck from thirty meters away.

I asked VanKamp why he tossed such a large training explosive.

"Didn't know it was going to explode like that!" He laughed.

A convoy of IPs met us a little farther down the road to see if we were okay. They could hear and feel the explosion from the police station.

The next day, we convoyed to the Husaybah Police Station for a quick visit. The Husaybah IPs recently located an American drone aircraft that was reported lost while on reconnaissance in June. The chief gave it to us, and we delivered the damaged drone to a

SEAL team that was also based at TQ with us on the north side. The SEALs had been looking for the lost drone for a few weeks. They were thankful for the find, but I credited the IPs. That was how close we were with the police. We also ran joint patrols with the IPs daily, mixing our gun trucks with their IP trucks. This showed the locals we worked as one. We became trusted by both, the locals and IPs. It was a great feeling to patrol within the police convoy through the many towns west of TQ. We also joined IP foot patrols along canals, schools, and neighborhoods.

With many signs of progress in May of 2007, congressman John Boehner said that only a "small residual of US Forces" should remain in Iraq beyond the end of 2011 with a scheduled withdrawal only. We were successful but needed to stay in the country that was still on the rebound. The surge was a true sign of success in Iraq. Prior to our unit's departure in October, Prime Minister Maliki managed to win a great deal of public support regarding US troops as trainers such as our 152nd Infantry in Iraq to keep stability in the country following possible withdrawals.

An active-duty army military police unit that was based near our headquarters on TQ north was planning to travel to Camp Ramadi but had never been there or convoyed to. I volunteered to ride along in their convoy. It was no problem at all. I'd get to see Captain Henton and others in the unit that I haven't seen in over two months since I was relocated at TQ north.

Traveling on Route Michigan from TQ to Ramadi for the first time was amazing. This was something impossible to attempt just a few weeks ago. Once nearing the city of Ramadi, I thought our convoy was lost. I was very familiar with Ar Ramadi, but something was odd. Were we lost? I recognized the main Ramadi mosque, and our convoy continued to roll west on what our tracking system showed was Route Michigan.

"This isn't it," I told the Hummer's driver. "We are not in Ramadi."

"The tracker says we are on the east side of Ramadi, sir," the driver replied. "On Route Michigan."

Ar Ramadi was different in every way. The bullet-ridden buildings were patched up, repaired, and painted. Local Iraqis were outside, shopping, riding bicycles, and cars were driving all over town, paying little or no attention to coalition convoys nearby. The people of Ar Ramadi felt safe and secure in their town once again. It was a remarkable feeling.

Jim Soriano was one of President Bush's provincial reconstruction team leaders in Iraq for the State Department.

"Things are starting to turn," Soriano stressed to the president during an October 2007 briefing of the surge and current situation in Iraq. "Something out here in Al Anbar is happening!"

Retired General Keane was in Iraq to assess the Iraqi situation and report directly to vice president Dick Cheney regarding the surge and its progress in early October. Keane's report to the vice president was welcomed with applause. Commander of the Iraqi Police, General Rahman Khaleed, agreed during the retired general's stunning remarks to the vice president.

"There is a significant shift in momentum" Keane proudly reported. Attacks against coalition forces were minimal. IEDs were basically unheard of. Choking the insurgent's fight with the surge proved successful, and the White House drew a much-needed sigh of relief.

President Bush would soon address the nation, stating, "The troop surge was working, and ordinary life is beginning to return" to the people of Iraq. The president confirmed that he would not replace two thousand marines in the Al Anbar Province set for return to the states. President Bush also ordered the return of one army combat brigade by Christmas of 2007.

Once our time was coming to a close in Iraq, our team wanted to do something for the Husaybah police officer's families. Sergeant VanKamp acquired a few truckloads of coloring books, crayons, pencils, soccer balls, and toys. We convoyed with a group of Iraqi Police trucks to the north side of Husaybah. That was an area that most of the IP's lived at with their families, and we wanted to hand the gifts out on the final mission during our one-year tour in Iraq.

Over one hundred Iraqi children swarmed our trucks that morning, and it was a huge hit. The kids loved us and, of course, treasured the gifts from the mysterious Americans who were proudly escorted by the police.

The surge was formally being recognized as a success, but our final days at TQ did not end well. One of the last missions our team completed was a typical four-vehicle convoy to visit a few IP checkpoints along Route Michigan, west of TQ. As our trucks rambled by a small village named Khalidia, I was told explosions could be easily seen to the north of our convoy.

Our convoy slowed, and a trio of IP trucks quickly responded to the area where the explosions were impacting. Mortars landed near a school on the outskirts of the Khalidia village that might have been meant for our convoy, destroying a playground. There were a few dozen Iraqi children in the area. Some were running away from the explosions while some stood in shock. Medium-sized mortars had hit the area that the children were playing near, killing a girl who only seemed eight or nine years old.

The IPs were desperate to locate the girl's family as our convoy provided security in the area, but the policemen could not identify the girl or her family.

Romeo quietly explained to me that the IPs were going to take the girl's body to the Hedaya Mosque, just on the other side of Route Michigan. The move had to be made due to the fact that the sun was ready to set soon in less than an hour.

Burial prior to sun set was very important in the Iraqi culture. Our trucks joined the IP convoy, and as we approached the masque, I feared the leadership of the community would think Americans killed the girl, specifically us.

Several Imams from the masque accepted the girl's body and quickly carried the girl into the building.

"I was worried they would challenge us," I said to Sergeant VanKamp.

"Me too," he replied with a sense of relief.

It was later confirmed that the mortar attack was meant for our convoy, but the attacker's aim was horrible. Someone set up a quick mortar piece, fired a dozen or so rounds quickly, and disappeared before being spotted.

Romeo reminded me of the bounty placed on my head by the insurgency. "The rounds were perhaps intended for you?" he added.

As the sun set that evening, I could not imagine what was going on at the masque with the unknown girl. It was heartbreaking.

During our team's highly anticipated convoy to our home base at Camp Ramadi, we rolled past the White Apartments for the last time. The apartments that could be seen on the right side of Michigan heading west on Route Michigan had been patched up since the earlier battles that reshaped the coalition effort in the region. A fresh new coat of mustard-yellow paint had just been added to the complex. I continued to wonder why the White Apartments were called this but strangely painted with a dark-mustard tint. Children could be seen playing in the courtyard. The apartment's parking lot that once was our staging area for Bradley Fighting Vehicles, Hummers, and IP trucks were now filled with cars. The gardens on both sides of the apartments were full and bright green with vegetables. Curtains in the windows of the White Apartments were waving in the breeze, and buses were leaving the parking lot of the nearby university, delivering students safely back to their homes in Ar Ramadi.

I ordered my driver to slow down; I needed to savor this moment and to take one last glance at the White Apartments as we banked north at Check Point Jones and headed to Ogden Gate. We did it, not our unit but the effort from all units and teams in the Anbar Province. Anbar was safe, and the awakening was successful.

Our wounded count was too high for me to remember. I stopped counting at one point of wounded that returned home from our tour during the surge. We had plenty of replacements who were attached to our unit to fill the wounded void. Some of the replacements were also injured, and some of the replacement's replacements were injured and sent home. I could not keep up with the number of injured during that year in Iraq. It was very difficult, the most difficult part of the deployment. It was very common to see new faces a few times each week who were attached to us. If not for the replacements who had been added to our unit, we could not have completed our mission. Some replacements came from the reserves, or they were in the inactive ready reserve that was known as the IRR prior to joining Team Cyclone. The soldiers plucked from the IRR were once active-duty army, reserve, or national guardsmen who were not on the active-duty roles or on current guard or reserve drilling status. The IRR was a very dangerous place to be in during the surge. They were called up and sent to units like ours.

Our number 2 mechanic, S.Sgt. Bradley King of La Fontaine, Indiana, was the company's only soldier to not survive our Iraqi combat tour. King was killed on April 2 during an attack in the northern Fallujah area of Al-A'amiriya. Officially, an IED strike killed Bradley, but I was told it was a rocket-propelled grenade strike that delivered the fatal wounds while Bradley was a rear passenger of a Humvee during a mission gone wrong. He was a great guy, fantastic mechanic, and bold soldier. He could fix anything and could fix anything with a smile. I miss him and think about him every day.

Bradley was survived by his wife and young son, several brothers, and a fantastic family who truly treasured him. At his funeral, his brothers could only smile of the stories I would tell them of Bradley in Iraq. He was an amazing guy and great soldier.

I damaged my right meniscus and tore my right calf muscle during a mission on the eastern side of Ramadi early during our tour. I also suffered three concussions during separate IED attacks while in Iraq. My third concussion knocked me out shortly. This happened on Route Mobile on the north east side of Fallujah. I credited our gun truck's survival to the jamming devices that were mounted on each of our vehicles that day near Fallujah. While in the trail vehicle of the east-bound convoy to Baghdad, a huge explosion rocked my Humvee as we passed the massive detonation. I know our jamming devices mounted on our gun trucks delayed the trigger. I blacked out, but everyone in the gun truck survived.

I missed the farewell ceremony that the First Armored Ready First held for our company of 152nd Cyclones. I went to Kuwait to welcome our unit's newest best friends, our much-anticipated replacements who would continue our effort with the Ar Ramadi Police. I did not keep up with soldiers from our replacement unit, an Army National Guard military police company from Kansas, but I hope they had the same success as we did, building close relationships with the Ramadi and Husaybah IPs and supporting the communities. I briefed our replacement company leadership of the Anbar Awakening and how the First Brigade senior leaders put everything on the line to make success work in the province known as Al Anbar.

I miss the time I had spent with my IP friends, setting up checkpoints along Route Michigan, eating perfectly cooked lamb, and enjoying fresh vegetables in the palace rotundum. I wish I could see them again or perhaps see them someday back here in America, Lieutenant Wathic, Sergeant Amar, my Iraqi interpreter Romeo, or whatever your real name was. Our memories are etched in my mind forever, and our comradery was unblemished.

The leadership of the inbound military police company unit absorbed each word during that morning's brief at Camp Virginia. The soldiers were relieved to hear from me that the Iraqi threat-level had nearly diminished as they had been told prior to arriving in Kuwait. I was able to speak with platoon leaders and platoon sergeants of what had evolved over the last year in the province and what life was like working with Iraqi Police.

Although stability was clearly seen and a drawdown was in work, a "status of forces agreement" with Iraqi National Security Advisor Mowaffak al-Rubaie was addressed to Condoleezza Rice and the White House. The agreement would mean that a large number of coalition forces should remain, and long-term American security was being sought by the Iraqi government following the surge.

AFTER THE SURGE

Overall, five US combat brigades to include support troops that added to about thirty thousand soldiers were surged into Iraq between February and June of 2007. Many of the surge effort focused on the Al Anbar Province, including us, a company from the Second Battalion of the 152nd Infantry Regiment. It was rewarding to see the accomplishments in the Al Anbar Province but a tough one for our gaggle of Indiana Army National Guard Infantrymen.

One week prior to our departure from Iraq, General Petraeus delivered the "Report to Congress on the Current Situation in Iraq." The four-star general explained that "military objectives of the surge are in large measure and are being met." Petraeus noted coalition forces have "disrupted Shia militia extremists," while capturing or killing high-target enemy leadership. As far as the Iraqi Police and Iraqi Army, Petraeus stated that "Iraqi (police) operations had drastically reduced ethno-sectarian violence in Iraq." The general also stressed to congress that a gradual drawdown of US Forces would be *premature*. I remember watching General Petraeus' brief and proud that the 152nd was a big factor in the surge's historic success.

Six weeks following our departure from Iraq, the decision was made to vacate Victory Base Complex, the huge stronghold near the Baghdad International Airport. Victory Base was the hub of the American war operation and housed the corps headquarters.

178

BATTLE OF THE WHITE APARTMENTS

US Forces had lost ninety-six in the ten-month period while we were based at Camp Ramadi compared to the follow-on units that relieved the First Brigade of "Old Ironsides" that lost four soldiers. Although suffering only a handful of losses, the effectiveness of the Anbar Awakening and the push to make the Iraqi Police stations successful was tremendous. The true contributing fact for the sharp declines of violence was the implementation of "concerned citizen" groups in the region conducting their own security and patrols in tribal areas, specifically the Iraqi Police.

This was our Infantry Company's 2006–2007 combat deployment as part of Operation Iraqi Freedom, a time during the Iraqi War known as "the surge." One of the shining symbols of counterinsurgency and warfighting that began with the historic "Anbar Awakening," spearheaded by Colonel MacFarland with Team Ready First, and this is a story of the surge.

Al-Jubouri, Najim Abdullah; Tal Afar Mayor
Al-Rishawi, Abdul Sattar Eftikhan;
Al Anbar Sheikh
Al-Rubaie, Mowaffak; Iraqi National Security Advisor
Al-Zarqawi, Abu Musab; Al-Qaeda Commander
Amar, Samir; Iraqi policeman and mechanic
Anrich, Jeff; Infantry Master Sergeant. Co. A, 152nd Infantry
Ashby, Thomas: USMC Gunnery Sergeant
Bennick, Terry; Infantry Lieutenant. Co. A, 152nd Infantry
Betnar, Justin; Sergeant, Co. A, 152nd Infantry Squad Leader
Boehner, John; US Congress Speaker of the House
Brawn, Jason; US Army Staff Sergeant. Co. A, 152nd Infantry
Bush, George W.; US President
Casey, William Jr.; US Army General
Casey, William Sr.; US Army Major General
Cheney, Dick; US Vice President
Chiarelli, Peter; US Lieutenant General
Denton, Ivan; US Army Major General, Indiana Army National Guard
Downs, James, USMC Captain
Eastwood, Clint; American actor, film director
Eller, Ronald; US Army Sergeant First Class, Co. A, 152nd Infantry
England, Lynndie; US Army, Military Police
Franks, Tommy; US Army General
Garrison, JB; Executive Officer. Co. A, 152nd Infantry
Garritt, Samual; IPLO Chief
Gates, Robert; Secretary of Defense
Gates, Teddy; US Marine Corps Major, First Armored Division,
    First Brigade
Gire, Richard, USMC Lt. Colonel
Gout, Robert, USMC Colonel
Graner, Charles; US Army, Military Police
Harvey, Derek; Middle East expert
Hastert, Dennis; US Speaker of the House
Henton, Daniel; Infantry Captain. Co. A, 152nd Infantry
Hobson, Nicky; US Army Staff Sergeant, Co. A, 152nd Infantry

Hussain, Saddam; Iraqi President

Johnson, Lyndon; US President

Kagan, Frederick; American Enterprise Institute

Kaddam, Yasin; Al Hurriya Iraqi Police Station Chief

Karpinski, Janis; Army Reserve Brigadier General

Keane, Jack; US Army General

Khaleed, Rahman; Iraqi Police General

King, Bradley; Staff Sergeant, Co. A, 152nd Infantry

Laddy, Marc; US Army Sergeant First Class, Co. A, 152nd Infantry

Lechner, Jim; Lieutenant Colonel, First Armored Division, Deputy Commander, First Brigade

MacFarland, Sean; Colonel, First Armored Division, Commander, First Brigade

Magruder, Bruce; Major General, First Armored Division

Al-Maliki, Nouri; Iraqi Prime Minister

McChrystal, Stanley; US Army General

McClung, Megan Malia Leilani; Reserve Major, United States Marine Corps

McMaster, HR; Army Lieutenant General

McNamara, Robert; Former US Secretary of Defense

Muhammad, Ahmad; Iraqi Police Major

North, Oliver; Reporter, Fox News, Retired Marine Lieutenant Colonel

Pace, Peter; US Marine Corps General, Chairman of the Joint Chiefs

Paterson, Joseph; Major General, Commander of training the Iraqi Police

Patriquin, Travis; Captain, US Army

Pelosi, Nancy; US Congress Speaker of the House

Perot, H. Ross, former presidential candidate

Petraeus, David, General, Commander US Forces in Iraq

Pomante, Vincent; Specialist, US Army

Ray, Richard; US Army Staff Sergeant. Co. A, 152nd Infantry

Reagan, Ronald; American President

Rice, Condoleezza; US Secretary of State

Rumsfeld, Donald; Secretary of Defense

Schwarzkopf, H. Norman; US Army General

Setton, Jacob; Specialist, Co. A, 152nd Infantry

Shannon, Patrick, Staff Sergeant, 152 Inf squad leader

Starnes, Chad; Infantry Lieutenant. Co. A, 152nd Infantry

Steele, William; Army Reserve Colonel, Commander, 451st Military Police Detachment

Tillman, Pat; US Army Ranger

Trump, Donald; US President

VanKamp, David; Sergeant First Class, Co. A, 152nd Infantry

Warner, John; US Senator

Wathic, Kaden; Lieutenant, Husaybah Iraqi Police

Wonka, Willie; fiction chocolate factory owner

ABOUT THE AUTHOR

A native of Indiana's Wabash Valley's small town of Greencastle, JB Garrison served as an infantry officer in the Indiana Army National Guard following graduation from the Indiana Military Officer Academy in 2003. An avid outdoorsman and bowhunter, Garrison is a proud graduate of Vincennes University earning an associate degree in general studies, later a bachelorette degree from Oakland City (Indiana) in business management, and eventually a graduate degree with Indiana Tech out of Fort Wayne in organizational management and leadership.

A proud American paratrooper, Garrison is a combat veteran of the invasion of Panama in 1989 during "Operation Just Cause" with the 82nd Airborne Division, also served during the Persian Gulf War's "Operation Desert Shield/Storm" in 1990 also with the 82nd, and was deployed to Yugoslavia in January of 1996 with the First Armored Division during "Operation Enduring Freedom" based in Tuzla, Bosnia. Following his 2006–2007 deployment, Garrison later returned to Iraq with the 219th Battlefield Surveillance Brigade as a brigade staff officer in 2011 before retiring from the military.

Garrison is currently a state employee with the Indiana Department of Corrections, serving the state as a senior parole agent. The author enjoys spending time with his grandson, Bronsyn, and hunting Indiana's treasured whitetail deer each fall in the thick woods of northern Putnam County, specifically the small town of Brick Chapel near "Cary Junction."

CPSIA information can be obtained
at www.ICGtesting.com
Printed in the USA
BVHW091947080322
630899BV00003B/366